TOEIC®: 2018 Format

Practice Tests 1–3

Andrew Betsis | Lawrence Mamas

INNOVA PRESS LIMITED
innova

Contents

Innova Press is an ELT publisher launched in 2017 with a mission to promote innovation in language education. We create readers, test preparation and practice materials and other titles in print and digital form based on the latest research in language education, with a specific focus on learner needs.

Published by Innova Press Ltd.
Suite 1, 3rd Floor, 11–12 St James's Square
London SW1Y 4LB
United Kingdom

ISBN 978-1-78768-039-5

British Library Cataloguing-in-Publication Data
A catalogue record for this book is available from the British Library.

The publishers wish to acknowledge the following use of material:
The photos in the Listening Sections © Ingram Publishing Image Library

Project management: Richard Peacock
Production and design: Global Blended Learning Ltd
Cover design: Becky Holland & Partners (BH&P)
Editorial: Lori Heaford
Audio recording: Global ELT recordings

This edition is not for sale in the following territories:

Cyprus
France
Greece
Hungary
Italy
Portugal
Spain

For sales in the following territories, please contact Innova Press Ltd.:

Indonesia
Poland
Romania
Taiwan
UAE
UK
Vietnam

Introduction

TOEIC® is an English-language test for EFL/ESL students. It tests the everyday English skills of people working in a global environment.

WHAT IS THE FORMAT OF THE TOEIC® TEST?

The test consists of **200 questions** divided into two sections. All the questions are in multiple-choice format. The total time is **two hours**.

Listening Section: The Listening Section tests how well you understand spoken English. It consists of four parts and contains 100 questions. Candidates are asked to answer questions based on a variety of statements, questions, conversations, and talks. Candidates must mark their answers on a separate answer sheet. They should not write their answers in their test book.
Total time: 45 minutes.

Reading Section: The Reading Section consists of three parts. Candidates have to read a variety of materials and answer 100 questions based on the materials provided to them. Candidates are encouraged to answer as many questions as possible within the time allowed. They must mark their answers on a separate answer sheet. They should not write their answers in their test book.
Total time: 75 minutes.

The TOEIC® test was revised in **2018**. The test time remains the same – 2 hours: 45 minutes for Listening and 75 minutes for Reading, the same paper and pencil administration, and the same range of difficulty as the previous test. The score scale is also the same.

TOEIC® OLD FORMAT	UPDATED 2018 TOEIC® FORMAT
Listening Comprehension 100 items	**Listening Comprehension 100 items**
Photographs: 10 questions	**Photographs:** 6 questions
Question–Response: 30 questions	**Question–Response:** 25 questions
Conversations: 30 questions: 10 conversations with 3 questions each	**Conversations:** 39 questions: 13 conversations with 3 questions each
Talks: 30 questions: 10 talks with 3 questions each	**Talks:** 30 questions: 10 talks with 3 questions each
Reading Comprehension 100 items	**Reading Comprehension 100 items**
Incomplete Sentences: 40 questions	**Incomplete Sentences:** 30 questions
Text Completion: 12 questions	**Text Completion:** 16 questions
Reading Comprehension: Single Passages: 28 questions: 7–10 reading texts with 2–5 questions each Double Passages: 20 questions: 4 pairs of reading texts with 5 questions per pair	**Reading Comprehension:** Single Passages: 29 questions: 10 reading texts with 2–4 questions each Multiple Passages: 25 questions: 5 sets of double or triple passages with 5 questions per set

2018 TOEIC® updates

The level of difficulty of the TOEIC® Listening and Reading test will remain the same, and the TOEIC® test will continue to be a fair, valid, and reliable exam of everyday and workplace English.

The score report will be the same, with the exception of one addition – Listening Ability Measured: understanding a speaker's purpose or implied meaning in a phrase or sentence. This provides additional information for test-takers and score users. The addition of the new Listening Ability Measured does not affect a test-taker's overall score. Scores will continue to be comparable across test administrations.

From what kind of contexts are the TOEIC® test questions drawn?

Offices: board meetings; committees; letters; memoranda; telephone, fax, and email messages; office equipment and furniture; office procedures

Personnel: recruiting, hiring, retiring, salaries, promotions, job applications, job advertisements, pensions, awards

Purchasing: shopping, ordering supplies, shipping, invoices

Technical Areas: electronics, technology, computers, laboratories and related equipment, technical specifications

Travel: trains, airplanes, taxis, buses, ships, ferries, tickets, schedules, station and airport announcements, car rentals, hotels, reservations, delays and cancelations

Corporate Development: research, product development

Dining Out: business and informal lunches, banquets, receptions, restaurant reservations

Entertainment: cinema, theater, music, art, exhibitions, museums, media

Finance and Budgeting: banking, investments, taxes, accounting, billing

General Business: contracts, negotiations, mergers, marketing, sales, warranties, business planning, conferences, labor relations

Health: medical insurance, visiting doctors, dentists, clinics, hospitals

Housing/Corporate Property: construction, specifications, buying and renting, electric and gas services

Manufacturing: assembly lines, plant management, quality control

Why take the TOEIC® test?

The TOEIC® test is the choice of nearly five million examinees a year and is recognized by many companies and governments all over the world.

What score do I need to "pass" the TOEIC® test?

TOEIC® is an English-language test designed specifically to measure the English skills of people working in an international environment. It is a score-based test, which means that you don't get a "pass mark" and you don't "fail".

It consists of 200 questions divided into 100 questions each in listening comprehension and reading comprehension. The candidates receive separate scores for the Listening and the Reading Sections on a scale from 5 to 495 points. The total score adds up to a scale from 10 to 990 points.

Preparing for the TOEIC® Test

It is very important to become familiar with the test format by doing a lot of Practice Tests in advance. The *TOEIC®: New Format Practice Tests* series consists of two books of three full-length TOEIC® Practice Tests and provides candidates with a total of 1,200 exam preparation questions. To get the most benefit from the Practice Tests, try to answer the questions within the time limits set for the actual tests.

Exam tips

- Answer ALL questions.
- Do not spend too much time on any one question.
- Mark your answers on your answer sheet.
- Be aware of the time limits. The test time is 2 hours: 45 minutes for the Listening Section and 75 minutes for the Reading Section.

Your score will be based on the number of questions you answer correctly. If you mark more than one answer, that question will be counted wrong, even if one of the answers is correct.

TOEIC®
PRACTICE
TESTS

Test 1

SECTION 1

Listening

In this section of the test, you will have the chance to show how well you understand spoken English. There are four parts to this section, with special directions for each part.

Part 1: Photographs

Directions: For each question, you will see a picture and you will hear four short statements. The statements will be spoken just one time. They will not be printed in your test book so you must listen carefully to understand what the speaker says. When you hear the four statements, look at the picture and choose the statement that best describes what you see in the picture. Choose the best answer (A), (B), (C), or (D).

EXAMPLE:

Now listen to the four statements. You will hear:

(A) He is on the phone.

(B) She is driving the car.

(C) She is typing on the computer.

(D) He is sitting next to her.

Statement (D) best describes what you see in the picture. Therefore, you should choose answer (D).

Sample Answer

A ☐ B ☐ C ☐ D ✔

1

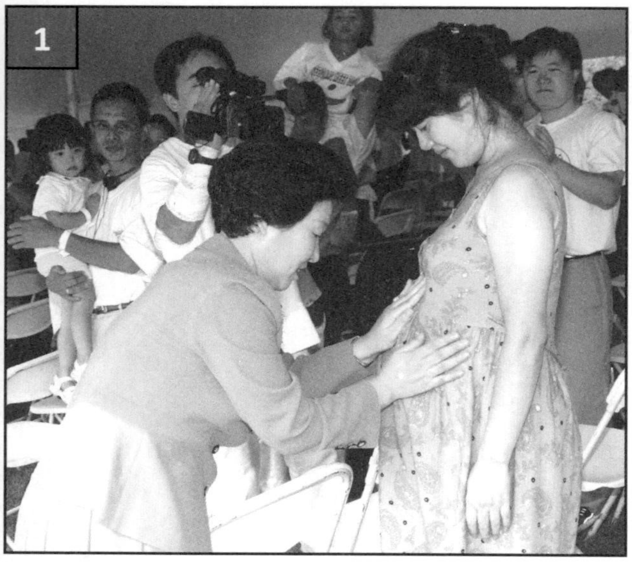

1. (A) ___ (B) ___ (C) ___ (D) ___

2

2. (A) ___ (B) ___ (C) ___ (D) ___

3

3. (A) ___ (B) ___ (C) ___ (D) ___

4

4. (A) ___ (B) ___ (C) ___ (D) ___

5. (A) ___ (B) ___ (C) ___ (D) ___

6. (A) ___ (B) ___ (C) ___ (D) ___

Part 2: Question–Response

Directions: In this part of the test, you will hear a question or statement spoken in English, followed by three responses, also spoken in English. The question or statement and the responses will be spoken just one time. They will not be printed in your test book, so you must listen carefully. You are to choose the best response to each question or statement. Now listen to a sample question.

You will hear: Man: Why are you late?

Woman: (A) I hope I won't be.

(B) My car broke down.

(C) He always is.

The best response is choice (B): "My car broke down". Therefore, you should choose (B).

7. (A)	(B)	(C)
8. (A)	(B)	(C)
9. (A)	(B)	(C)
10. (A)	(B)	(C)
11. (A)	(B)	(C)
12. (A)	(B)	(C)
13. (A)	(B)	(C)
14. (A)	(B)	(C)
15. (A)	(B)	(C)
16. (A)	(B)	(C)
17. (A)	(B)	(C)
18. (A)	(B)	(C)
19. (A)	(B)	(C)
20. (A)	(B)	(C)
21. (A)	(B)	(C)
22. (A)	(B)	(C)
23. (A)	(B)	(C)
24. (A)	(B)	(C)
25. (A)	(B)	(C)
26. (A)	(B)	(C)
27. (A)	(B)	(C)
28. (A)	(B)	(C)
29. (A)	(B)	(C)
30. (A)	(B)	(C)
31. (A)	(B)	(C)

Part 3: Conversations

Directions: You will hear some conversations between two or more people. You will be asked to answer three questions about what the speakers say in each conversation. Select the best response to each question and mark the letter (A), (B), (C), or (D) on your answer sheet. The conversations will not be printed in your test book and will be spoken only one time.

32. How does Megan feel about the presentation she will give?
(A) confident (C) terrified
(B) unsure (D) proud

33. What is true about Megan?
(A) She is advising Michael.
(B) She is preparing at the last minute.
(C) She is planning ahead.
(D) She has been to a lot of conferences.

34. What will happen on Friday the 5th?
(A) Michael will help Megan.
(B) Megan will give a presentation.
(C) Michael has a deadline.
(D) There is a conference.

35. What is the woman trying to do?
(A) earn some money in the summer
(B) get help for a disabled child
(C) offer her assistance
(D) meet Anna

36. What does the woman need to do next?
(A) come back in a few hours
(B) come back any morning
(C) try to find another place to volunteer
(D) give the man her CV

37. How could the man be best described?
(A) helpful (C) afraid
(B) unhelpful (D) annoyed

38. How does the woman feel?
(A) exhausted
(B) impatient
(C) grateful
(D) annoyed

39. Why did the man make a mistake?
(A) He was careless.
(B) He did not have information.
(C) He wanted to provoke the woman.
(D) The job was complex.

40. Why couldn't the woman go on Thursday evening?
(A) Elsie told her that she must not.
(B) She will miss the meeting.
(C) She has to work.
(D) She just doesn't want to.

41. What would the woman like to be doing on the weekend?
(A) visiting Todd (C) working on a computer
(B) swimming (D) taking a sick day

42. What is the tone of the man's words?
(A) angry (C) joking
(B) serious (D) regretful

43. What is the relationship between the three speakers?
(A) family members (C) employees and boss
(B) coworkers (D) friends

44. Why does the woman say, "Yes, most of us are struggling."?
(A) She can't accept the man's decision.
(B) She tries to make the man work harder.
(C) She feels guilty about what they have to do.
(D) She wants to show understanding.

45. What was the purpose of the man's conversation with Ms Johnson?
(A) to give information (C) to get sympathy
(B) to ask for help (D) to challenge her

46. What is the relationship between the man and Ms Johnson?
(A) relatives (C) friends
(B) coworkers (D) employee and boss

47. What does the woman imply when she says, "Her eyes were sparkling and she had a huge smile!"?
(A) Laura was really beautiful that day.
(B) Laura was excited about the job offered to her.
(C) Laura was really happy to see the woman.
(D) Laura was very happy in her current job.

48. What does the woman think Laura will do?
(A) She will definitely take the job.
(B) She will definitely not take the job.
(C) She will probably take the job.
(D) She will not be able to decide.

49. Why does the man think it would be hard for Laura to decide to take the job?
(A) It is not a good position.
(B) It is far from her family.
(C) She is not adventurous.
(D) She must decide quickly.

50. How did the man feel when he heard about the woman's decision?
(A) worried
(B) frustrated
(C) surprised
(D) annoyed

51. How often does the woman think she would use the car?
(A) every day
(B) occasionally
(C) constantly
(D) very rarely

52. What does the man think is the problem with renting a car?
(A) It would be too expensive.
(B) It would interfere with work.
(C) It would discourage trips.
(D) It would be unnecessary.

53. How is the woman feeling?
(A) disappointed
(B) frightened
(C) worried
(D) relaxed

54. Why is the woman unhappy with her office mate?
(A) She is obnoxious.
(B) She doesn't answer her questions.
(C) She doesn't start conversations.
(D) She bothers her all the time.

55. How does the man think the woman should be?
(A) straightforward
(B) independent
(C) cautious
(D) confrontational

56. What food does the man not like?
(A) steak
(B) chips
(C) salad
(D) tomato

57. If the man doesn't eat his salad, what will happen?
(A) He will go hungry.
(B) He will still eat well.
(C) He will let someone down.
(D) It will be the end of the world.

58. How can the woman be described?
(A) bored
(B) indifferent
(C) delighted
(D) polite

59. What is the man's job?
(A) to design things
(B) to make things
(C) to sell things
(D) to invent things

60. What was the man's attitude towards his work?
(A) He enjoyed it.
(B) He worked hard but didn't like it.
(C) It was not very important to him.
(D) He was serious and practical.

61. Why is the woman speaking to the man?
(A) to warn him about a job
(B) to thank him for his work
(C) to encourage him to work harder
(D) to ask for his assistance.

WEEK	TYPE OF PROPERTY	CLIENT
last week	condo	Mr and Mrs Jenkins
	beachfront bungalow	Mr and Mrs Jones
this week	townhouse	Mr and Ms Phillips
next week	1-bedroom city apartment	
	single-family home	
	downtown loft	Mr and Mrs Lewis

62. Look at the graphic. Who is currently interested in buying some property?
(A) Mr and Mrs Phillips
(B) Mr and Mrs Jones
(C) Mr and Mrs Lewis
(D) Mr and Mrs Jenkins

63. How does the man feel?
(A) depressed
(B) reluctant
(C) disappointed
(D) scared

64. Where is the woman going now?
(A) back home
(B) the cafe
(C) the canteen
(D) the store

65. Which department do the speakers work in?

(A) management
(B) finance
(C) design
(D) administration

66. What is the woman's attitude towards the managers?

(A) considerate
(B) disrespectful
(C) sympathetic
(D) excited

67. How does the man feel?

(A) tired
(B) frustrated
(C) relaxed
(D) sad

PROPERTY	LOCATION	PRICE
single-family home	countryside	300,000
townhouse	suburbs	200,000
condo	downtown	250,000
townhouse	riverfront	180,000

68. How did the first man feel when he heard about the woman's decision?

(A) surprised
(B) angry
(C) disinterested
(D) unhappy

69. Look at the graphic. Which property are they discussing?

(A) the house in the countryside
(B) the downtown condo
(C) the riverfront townhouse
(D) the suburban house

70. What does Bill think the woman should do?

(A) spend more money
(B) buy the house they've just seen
(C) forget about the location and concentrate on the house
(D) rethink their priorities

Part 4: Talks

Directions: You will hear some talks given by a single speaker. You will be asked to answer three questions about what the speaker says in each talk. Select the best response to each question and mark the letter (A), (B), (C), or (D) on your answer sheet. The talks will not be printed in your test book and will be spoken only one time.

71. What is the building?

(A) a factory (C) a gallery
(B) a shop (D) a hospital

72. What were the Bradford family?

(A) artists (C) actors
(B) politicians (D) fashion designers

73. Who is Charles Bradford?

(A) Alan's great-grandfather
(B) an artist visiting the opening
(C) an artist
(D) a classical music player

DEPARTURE	DESTINATION	TRAIN NUMBER
11.15	Washington	78596
10.50	Washington	78459
11.30	Atlanta	58963
11.40	Atlanta	58942

74. What has affected the 10.50 train to Washington?

(A) There was no driver.
(B) It had broken down.
(C) There was a signal failure.
(D) There were passengers on the track.

75. Look at the graphic. Which one of these trains is an express one?

(A) 58963 (C) 78596
(B) 78459 (D) 58942

76. Which platform will the Washington train leave from?

(A) 6 (C) 11
(B) 7 (D) 4

77. Who is talking?

(A) a receptionist (C) a waiter
(B) a shop assistant (D) a butcher

78. How many specials are there to choose from?

(A) four (C) three
(B) five (D) two

79. What does he not tell them about immediately?

(A) the fish (C) the desserts
(B) the steak (D) the salads

80. Who is the talk directed at?

(A) campaigners (C) politicians
(B) radio listeners (D) astronomers

81. By what percentage has light pollution increased over the last 10 years?

(A) 25% (C) 11%
(B) 10% (D) 5%

82. What is the next thing the listeners will hear?

(A) an astronomer (C) music
(B) Mervin (D) horoscopes

83. How many films will be shown this week?

(A) three

(B) seven

(C) twelve

(D) two

84. Why does the speaker say, "The film will break even the hardest heart."?

(A) to prevent children from watching

(B) to criticize the film's main idea

(C) to warn people with heart problems

(D) to show how emotional the film is

85. What will happen after the film?

(A) There will be refreshments.

(B) The director will make a speech.

(C) The actors will perform.

(D) The cast will go to a wine bar.

---

86. Why does the speaker say, "Attention, shoppers!"?

(A) Shoppers must beware of their personal belongings.

(B) There has been a change in opening times.

(C) Customers should be aware of available discounts.

(D) A child has gone missing.

87. Where can you get something free to eat?

(A) KidsWorld

(B) The Coffee Place

(C) the bakery

(D) the supermarket

88. What time is it now?

(A) 5 p.m.

(B) 3 p.m.

(C) 4 p.m.

(D) 8 p.m.

89. Where are they?

(A) on the plane on the runway

(B) in the airport building

(C) on the bus

(D) in a plane in the air

90. Who is speaking?

(A) a member of the ground crew

(B) a member of the cabin crew

(C) the captain

(D) a luggage handler

91. Look at the graphic. What time are they departing from London?

(A) 8.10

(B) 7.30

(C) 7.00

(D) 7.50

	Departure (GMT)	Arrival local time: (GMT + 1 hour)
London – Paris		09.10
Paris – Cairo		
Cairo – Cape Town		

---

92. What is the problem?

(A) A computer is not working.

(B) A computer did not arrive.

(C) Someone needs to find a service center.

(D) A telephone is not working.

93. The man speaking is

(A) on the radio.

(B) at the computer.

(C) at home.

(D) on the telephone.

94. What should be done first?

(A) Click the 'my computer' icon.

(B) Click the 'programs' icon.

(C) Connect to the internet.

(D) Close all programs.

95. Who is most likely speaking?

(A) a store owner

(B) a radio announcer

(C) a professor

(D) someone who read a newspaper

96. What is predicted to happen in two years' time?

(A) a recession

(B) the dollar will rise against the yen

(C) a housing slump

(D) interest rates will be cut

97. What accounts for two-thirds of the US economy?

(A) consumer spending

(B) housing

(C) banking

(D) investment

---

98. Who is being spoken to?

(A) staff at registration

(B) delegates

(C) a presenter

(D) a conference organizer

99. How many times has this conference taken place before?

(A) four

(B) one

(C) zero

(D) two

100. What happens at 9 a.m. tomorrow?

(A) registration begins

(B) delegates arrive

(C) presentations begin

(D) breakfast

Vocabulary Development for Test 1, Reading, Parts 5 & 6

nevertheless: (adv) despite that

eligibility (n): the state of being able to do something because you are in the right situation

candidacy (n): being a candidate in an election

bankruptcy (n): being declared in law as unable to pay your debts

bail (n): money that someone agrees to pay to release someone from jail

rectify (v): to correct something that is wrong

flourish (v): to develop well

enlightenment (n): the understanding of something

rip (n): a tear in cloth or paper

spam (n): an unwanted advertising email

inclination (n): a desire to do something

lapse (n): a mistake, especially one that happens because of carelessness

digression (n): talking about something that is not related to what you were talking about before

morbid (adj): interested in unpleasant things, such as death

marginal (adj): small and unimportant

menial (adj): (of work) boring and unimportant, often badly paid

invigorate (v): to make someone feel energetic and fresh

incensed (adj): very angry

inhale (v): to take something into your lungs as you breathe

comprehend (v): to understand

fondness (n): a feeling of pleasure or enjoyment from something you like

Vocabulary Development for Test 1, Reading, Parts 5 & 6

Exercise A

Choose the correct answer, (A), (B), or (C), to complete the sentences.

1. After the accident, all the people who had .... the fumes were taken to hospital.
   (A) inhaled
   (B) invigorated
   (C) flourished
2. You need to check your .... for unemployment benefit.
   (A) enlightenment
   (B) inclination
   (C) eligibility
3. He .... his candidacy for the post.
   (A) flourished
   (B) announced
   (C) inhaled
4. She said that her old job was .... work, such as washing dishes and cleaning floors.
   (A) menial
   (B) incensed
   (C) morbid

Exercise B

Choose the correct word, (A), (B), or (C), to fill the gaps in the text.

After several **(5)** ...., she finally got to the point. She said that it was her father's **(6)** .... for drink that brought about the break-up of her parents' marriage. Her little brother was too young to **(7)** .... what was happening, but she said with her it was different as it had affected her very badly.

5. (A) rips (B) digressions (C) spams
6. (A) fondness (B) enlightenment (C) bail
7. (A) comprehend (B) invigorate (C) inhale

Exercise C

Complete the sentences using the correct form of three of the words in the box below.

invigorate	morbid	marginal	incensed	lapse
bail	nevertheless	bankruptcy	enlightenment	rip

8. Workers were .... by the decision to lengthen working hours and they started talking about protesting.
9. I am not happy about the story as it will only be of .... interest to our readers.
10. She asked me to give her some .... on what happened.

Practice Test 1

SECTION 2

Reading

In the Reading test, you will read a variety of texts and answer several different types of reading comprehension questions. The entire Reading test will last 75 minutes. There are three parts, and directions are given for each part. You are encouraged to answer as many questions as possible within the time allowed. You must mark your answers on the separate answer sheet. Do not write your answers in your test book.

Part 5: Incomplete Sentences

Directions: A word or phrase is missing in each of the sentences below. Four answer choices are given below each sentence. Select the best answer to complete the sentence. Then mark the letter (A), (B), (C), or (D) on your answer sheet.

Example: Her boss was talking to her ....
(A) angry (B) friendly (C) angrily (D) unfriendly Correct answer: (C)

101. .... John found his manager hard to get along with, he did the best he could.
(A) So difficult (C) Nevertheless
(B) Because of (D) Although

102. He was forced to declare .... two years after purchasing the property for his business because he couldn't make the payments.
(A) eligibility (C) bankruptcy
(B) candidacy (D) bail

103. Although his new job had long hours, Mike was pleased with his higher ....
(A) dues (C) fees
(B) salary (D) earns

104. Be sure to submit your application form by the 20th of March .... you wish to be considered for the post.
(A) unless that (C) if
(B) whether (D) in case of

105. I .... the report now; I'll be with you in a second.
(A) finish (C) would finish
(B) finished (D) am finishing

106. The day of the meeting has been changed; it has been .... for Thursday.
(A) reserved (C) rectified
(B) cancelled (D) rescheduled

107. On one hand, we've had a bit of a setback, but on .... hand, it's a chance to show that we're determined to make this business flourish again.
(A) the other (C) the second
(B) another (D) that

108. Be sure to let me know if I can be of any ....
(A) assistance (C) inclination
(B) enlightenment (D) clarification

109. Due to a .... in security, hackers got access to the company's files.
(A) rebate (C) spam
(B) rip (D) lapse

110. Lunch .... after the meeting, when you will have a chance to have an informal chat with the new boss.
(A) will serve (C) will be served
(B) to be served (D) is serving

111. Although one of the two candidates has more experience, ... has great enthusiasm and energy.
(A) either (C) another
(B) the one (D) the other

112. The bus is departing .... so please hurry up, otherwise you will be late for work.
(A) promptly (C) prompted
(B) prompt (D) prompting

113. Does the position include any ...., such as a company car or health insurance?

(A) bonuses (C) breaks

(B) benefits (D) brackets

114. Many were worried the country would suffer a .... because of the rise in interest rates.

(A) digression (C) recession

(B) regression (D) depletion

115. The folder .... you will find the report is on the top shelf.

(A) which (C) where is

(B) in which (D) wherever

116. It is important that you .... any concerns you might have so we can address them.

(A) rally (C) rage

(B) raise (D) rule

117. She doesn't like wearing a uniform at work. She is the kind of person who likes to dress to ....

(A) impress (C) impressive

(B) impressed (D) impressively

118. Michelle felt like she was kept on the .... and was not really considered part of the team.

(A) outline (C) off line

(B) sidelines (D) guidelines

119. Amy decided to .... in cardiology after graduating from medical school.

(A) investigate (C) explore

(B) detail (D) specialize

120. The hierarchy .... the company was very complex.

(A) within (C) around

(B) on (D) among

121. Anna was concerned about keeping her job because the company was ....

(A) expanding (C) downsizing

(B) condensing (D) backdating

122. Profits were ....; better than last year, but still short of our goal.

(A) morbid (C) menial

(B) marginal (D) meaningless

123. I'm afraid I'm ....; I've been working in the office since 7 a.m.

(A) exhausted (C) extended

(B) invigorated (D) incensed

124. Mario felt that he did not get enough .... for his hard work.

(A) recognition (C) consideration

(B) stimulation (D) obligation

125. Alison, like her sister Jessica, ... studying to be a lawyer.

(A) also (C) are

(B) have been (D) is

126. I would like to thank you for your .... in reaching a speedy solution to the unexpected problems of the merging of the two businesses.

(A) reluctance (C) inclination

(B) cooperation (D) resistance

127. Ann .... to attend an interview for the position of Assistant Director on Thursday.

(A) is going (C) has been

(B) goes (D) had been

128. .... you were working under pressure, you have done an excellent job!

(A) However (C) In spite of

(B) Although (D) No wonder

129. The check .... because the account was empty and he was charged a fee.

(A) failed (C) slid

(B) rolled (D) bounced

130. In order to be efficient, you must .... on the task at hand.

(A) strive (C) aim

(B) focus (D) grasp

Part 6: Text Completion

Directions: Read the texts that follow. A word or phrase is missing in some of the sentences. Four answer choices are given below each of the sentences. Select the best answer to complete the text. Then mark the letter (A), (B), (C), or (D) on your answer sheet.

Questions 131–134 refer to the following memo.

MEMO

To: **All Employees**
From: **Jane Anderson, Personnel**
Date: **Thursday 29 Oct**
Subject: **CHARITY BARBECUE**

Just a reminder that the charity barbecue is happening this Friday! It is for a good cause: we're .... money for the children's' charity *Future Horizons* to buy computers for community centers in disadvantaged neighborhoods, so please come along and help out!

131. (A) taking (B) raising (C) earning (D) giving

It will be at 7.30 at Oak Park, next to the gazebo by the west gate. Dinner will be 15 dollars and there will be hamburgers, hotdogs, or veggie burgers and, of course, lots of salads and desserts! Bring your family and friends; everyone is welcome. ....

132. (A) Please get tickets from me or from Sophia Johnson.
(B) Why wouldn't you; it's free anyway!
(C) Children are not allowed on the premises.
(D) Attendance is mandatory for all employees.

I hope .... you there!
Jane Anderson

133. (A) to see (B) will see (C) seeing (D) to seeing

PS. .... bad weather, there will be a marquee erected in the park.

134. (A) As there was (B) Despite the (C) In case of (D) Especially with

Questions 135–138 refer to the following leaflet.

WHAT IS TUBERCULOSIS?

Tuberculosis is a bacterial disease which causes infection, most commonly in the lungs, but .... in other body organs. It is transmitted by inhaling bacteria coughed or sneezed into the air by infected persons.

135. (A) more commonly
(B) nevertheless
(C) never
(D) occasionally

WHAT IS A MANTOUX TEST?

A substance called tuberculin is injected into the skin on the forearm to find out whether or not there are tuberculosis bacteria present in the body.

HOW IS THE TEST ANALYZED?

48 to 72 hours after the injection, the forearm is examined. For most individuals, a swelling that measures 10mm or more .... that the person has been in contact with tuberculosis. This is a positive result.

136. (A) involves (B) indicates (C) inclines (D) induces

No reaction, or only slight redness or bruising, suggests that the person has not been in contact with tuberculosis. This is a negative result.

PEOPLE REQUIRING MANTOUX TESTS:

Mantoux tests may .... for new employees, volunteers, residents, and clients of some organizations and institutions. All people who have .... in contact with a person with active tuberculosis should be tested as soon as possible, and again, three months after the date of last contact.

137. (A) be required (B) be requiring (C) required (D) are required

138. (A) taken (B) come (C) had (D) gone

Questions 139–142 refer to the following email.

From: **Mary Richardson**
To: **Terrence Jones**
Cc:
Subject: **Job Opening**

Mr Jones,
I am emailing to bring to your attention the opening in our department that is advertised on our website. I would like to recommend that you .... applying, since the work that you have already done for our company on a freelance basis makes you highly .... for the position.

139. (A) withhold
(B) retract
(C) comprehend
(D) consider

140. (A) talented
(B) inclined
(C) invited
(D) qualified

The job offers quite flexible working hours, as .... comprehensive health benefits. If you have any questions or would like more information, please feel .... to contact me by email or at 2477755674 Ext: 239.

Regards,
Mary Richardson, Personnel

141. (A) such
(B) some
(C) well as
(D) plenty

142. (A) loose
(B) released
(C) liberal
(D) free

Questions 143–146 refer to the following advertisement.

JOB VACANCY

Online Marketing Technician

.... This person will be .... in our Auckland, NZ, office, will manage a range of email marketing, and will lead generation campaigns for our growing list of clients. Salary to be discussed.

143. (A) We are sorry to announce our Marketing Manager has resigned.
(B) Our company has long been the best in its field.
(C) We offer a part-time unpaid internship job.
(D) I am on the job hunt for another team member.

144. (A) replaced
(B) based
(C) homed
(D) found

You will need to be proficient in HTML, have a fondness for detail and like working on a variety of projects.

This role will suit .... who have a few years' work experience in web development with some client-facing involvement and can show an ability and desire to uncover all there is to know about online marketing.

145. (A) who
(B) those
(C) them
(D) whoever

If you are interested in knowing more, then it is probably best to use the sales .... form to kick things off.

146. (A) inquiring
(B) inquire
(C) inquiry
(D) inquirer

Vocabulary Development for Test 1, Reading, Part 7

accommodate (v): to give someone a place to live

quintessential: (adj) representing the most perfect or typical example of something

assortment (n): different types of something grouped together

exquisite (adj): extremely beautiful and delicate

crescendo (n): a gradual increase in excitement or loudness

acclaimed (adj): publicly praised

recruit (v): to convince someone to work for a company or to become a member of an organization

confine (v): to limit something

evacuate (v): to empty a place because of danger

unobstructed: (adj) clear, with no obstacles

dispatcher (n): a person whose job is to send people out to where they are needed, especially to emergencies

intention (n): something that you plan to do

distinct (adj): clearly visible

stimulate (v): to encourage something

lure (v): to persuade or trick someone into doing something by offering them something exciting

liaison (n): a communication link that connects people or groups

unsolicited (adj): not asked for

insert (n): something that is made to go inside something else

defrost (v): to become no longer frozen

rustic (adj): something that appears simple and rough in appearance, typical of the countryside

clientele (n): all the customers of a business

competent (adj): having the skill to do something well

aggregation (n): the act of putting together several amounts of things

Vocabulary Development for Test 1, Reading, Part 7

Exercise A

Choose the correct answer, (A), (B), or (C), to complete the sentences.

1. The single-profit figure is a(n) .... of many, and it is earned from completely different markets.

(A) aggregation

(B) clientele

(C) crescendo

2. The law firm has an elite ....

(A) liaison

(B) clientele

(C) assortment

3. The sales chart shows a(n) .... decline in the past few months.

(A) distinct

(B) unobstructed

(C) quintessential

4. The new manager's office was decorated in .... taste.

(A) unsolicited

(B) exquisite

(C) competent

Exercise B

Choose the correct word, (A), (B), or (C), to fill the gaps in the text.

Laura was fed up with city life and decided to move to the countryside. She looked at various estate agents' websites and, after six months of viewings, she finally bought an old cottage full of **(5)** .... charm in a **(6)** .... village in the south-west of England. She now wanted to focus on her writing. Laura was a(n) **(7)** .... writer – she was very creative and people of all ages loved her stories.

5.	(A) acclaimed	(B) unsolicited	(C) rustic
6.	(A) quintessential	(B) competent	(C) unsolicited
7.	(A) rustic	(B) competent	(C) unobstructed

Exercise C

Complete the sentences using the correct form of three of the words in the box below.

defrost	insert	stimulate	evacuate	dispatcher
liaison	crescendo	assortment	lure	accommodate

8. Workers were .... by the decision to lengthen working hours, and they started talking about protesting.

9. I am not happy about the story as it will only be of .... interest to our readers.

10. She asked me to give her some .... on what happened.

Part 7: Reading Comprehension

Directions: You will read a selection of texts, such as magazine and newspaper articles, letters, and advertisements. Each text is followed by several questions. Select the best answer for each question and mark the letter (A), (B), (C), or (D) on your answer sheet.

Example: Are you someone who enjoys trying new things and does not feel uncomfortable in new environments? Then why not get paid for it? *CULTURE* magazine is looking for individuals to go to new clubs, events, etc., and write about the cultural scene they observe in these places. Interested? Send your resume to CULTURE@hotmail.com. Please, no phone calls.

What type of person would be best qualified for this job?

(A) a homebird (B) an introvert (C) a clumsy person (D) a risk-taker Correct answer: (D)

Questions 147–148 refer to the following card.

In case of an emergency, if oxygen levels in the cabin become too low, an oxygen mask will be automatically released from the area above your head. Pull the mask gently towards you to begin the flow of oxygen. The bag will not fully inflate. Always put on your own mask before attempting to help others.

147. Where would this card most likely be found?

(A) on a train
(B) in an office
(C) on an airplane
(D) in a hotel room

148. Which of the following actions are correct?

(A) Call for assistance if the bag does not inflate.
(B) Remove the mask from a compartment above you.
(C) Put on your child's mask and then your own.
(D) Carefully pull the mask downward.

Questions 149–151 refer to the following advertisement.

RESERVATIONS

To ensure a table at SkyCity, at the top of Seattle's *Space Needle*, reservations are recommended. To make a reservation call: 206-905-2100 or 800-937-9582.

Corporate groups are welcome but must be scheduled in advance and are limited to no more than 21 guests. Parties of 10 or more cannot be accommodated May 31 through September 3.

Your elevator ride and Observation Deck visit are complimentary with your reservation at SkyCity.

Reservations are available for seating during the following hours:

Lunch	Monday–Friday:	11.00 a.m.–3.00 p.m.	
Brunch	Saturday & Sunday:	10.00 a.m.–3.00 p.m.	
Dinner	Sunday–Thursday:	5.00 p.m.–9.00 p.m.	Friday & Saturday: 5.00 p.m.–10.00 p.m.

149. What kind of a place is SkyCity?

(A) a restaurant
(B) a ship
(C) a museum
(D) a theme park

150. When could you go with a party of 12 people?

(A) February 2nd, without needing a reservation
(B) June 24th, with a reservation
C) May 3rd, with a reservation
(D) You cannot go with a group of 12 people.

151. What time on Friday can you NOT reserve a table?

(A) 10 a.m.
(B) 2 p.m.
(C) 9 p.m.
(D) 9.30 p.m.

Sydney Opera House High Tea

Australia's celebrated chef Guillaume Brahimi, Michelin-trained with Two Chef Hats, has created a sophisticated High Tea in quintessential Sydney style.

You will be welcomed with a glass of fine Australian sparkling wine, then presented with an assortment of beautiful teas, exquisite savories, pastries, and petit fours.

The crescendo of this perfect Sydney afternoon is an intimate and private performance by an acclaimed opera singer that will leave you entranced. Perfect for entertaining important clients.

High Teas are from 2 p.m.–4 p.m. on the following dates:

Wed. 10 October
Wed. 24 October
Wed. 7 November
Wed. 21 November
Wed. 5 December
Wed. 2 January
Wed. 9 January
Wed. 16 January
Wed. 23 January
Wed. 30 January
Wed. 6 February
Wed. 13 February
Wed. 20 February
Wed. 27 February

Bookings are essential.
Call: +61 2 9250 7250
Email: tourism@sydneyoperahouse.com **Cost: $145 per person**

152. What is the purpose of this leaflet?

(A) to attract customers
(B) to promote Australian wine
(C) to give a warning
(D) to recruit employees

153. What is not included in the event?

(A) coffee
(B) live music
(C) food
(D) alcohol

154. Which of the following statements is most accurate?

(A) You can't book in advance.
(B) You don't have to book in advance.
(C) You might not be able to book in advance.
(D) You must book in advance.

Questions 155–157 refer to the following email.

To:	**All Employees**
From:	**Jason Byrne**
CC:	**Brian Weston**
Subject:	**Software Training Session**
Attachments:	

I'm sending this out to remind everyone that we are holding Software Training Sessions this Friday in the Computer Lab. There will be a morning session and an afternoon session, so be sure to sign up for your preference in the IT office if you haven't already. Each session should take about four hours.

I'm sure you realize the importance of these sessions, as there has been considerable discussion of our company's decision to change from the Windows to Linux running system, and concern about making a smooth transition. I want to say again that we are not expecting any difficulties. *Utrans* is a very user-friendly program. Dr Brian Weston will be doing the training, and you will be in good hands.

Jason Byrne, Manager, IT Department

155. What is the email's purpose?

(A) an announcement

(B) a reminder

(C) a warning

(D) a guide

156. How do employees know which session to go to?

(A) They just turn up when they can.

(B) They ask at the IT office.

(C) They are informed in the email.

(D) They choose themselves.

157. Approximately, how much of the workday does each training session fill?

(A) all day

(B) half a day

(C) a couple of hours

(D) approximately four minutes

Questions 158–160 refer to the following notice.

FIRE PROCEDURE IN THE WORKPLACE

If you detect FIRE or SMOKE, do this at once:

1. STAY CALM and use common sense.
2. Close the door to CONFINE the fire and smoke. **-[1]-**
3. ACTIVATE THE FIRE ALARM – a small red box located on the wall near each office exit. Follow the instructions on the alarm. **-[2]-**
4. REPORT THE FIRE. Call the UAB on 911 or use the HELP PHONE, identify yourself, and tell the dispatcher the exact location of the fire or smoke and what is burning. **-[3]-**
5. EVACUATE. All building occupants should proceed to the nearest exit, move away from the building, and assemble in a location predetermined by your supervisor. **-[4]-** It is also important that the Fire Department has clear and unobstructed access to the building.

158. During a fire, why should you close doors?

(A) to demonstrate that you are calm

(B) to help facilitate evacuation

(C) to give the Fire Department clear access

(D) to stop the fire from spreading

159. What is NOT mentioned as something that you should tell the dispatcher after dialing 911?

(A) who you are

(B) where the fire is

(C) what is on fire

(D) how the fire started

160. In which of the positions marked [1], [2], [3], and [4] does the following sentence best belong?
"This will provide a quick and easy way to account for all personnel."

(A) [1]

(B) [2]

(C) [3]

(D) [4]

Practice Test 1

Questions 161–163 refer to the following letter.

August 29th

The Manager
Travelsafe Insurance
217 26th Ave
Portland, Oregon 76634

Policy No. R3990007
Valid up to: August 1st

Dear Sir or Madam,

This is to bring to your notice that my luggage, insured with your office under the above-mentioned travel insurance policy, was lost on August 12th on a flight from New York to Spain with Globetrotter Airlines.

Because the luggage was lost at the beginning of a company team-building trip, it was necessary to replace it. This included clothing, personal items, and camping and climbing equipment. Enclosed, please find an estimate of replacement costs.

Yours truly,
James A. Witman

161. What is the purpose of this letter?

(A) to report an insurance payout

(B) to acquire travel insurance

(C) to make an insurance claim

(D) to respond to a question

162. When does this insurance policy expire?

(A) 12th August of this year

(B) 29th August of this year

(C) 1st August of next year

(D) 12th August of next year

163. What item did Mr Witman NOT have to replace?

(A) sleeping bag

(B) laptop

(C) trousers

(D) climbing ropes

Question 164–166 refer to the following timetable.

Travel information for { Mrs Browning } for { Friday's } company meeting

Departure station	CTS	CTS	CTS	CTS	CTS
Train number	V344	G56	G983	HJ89	G211
Arrival station	MCT	MCT	MCT	MCT	MCT
Departs	08.14	09.22	09.47	09.51	10.22
Arrives	13.39	14.05	14.39	14.39	15.05
Duration	5:25	4.43	4.52	4.48	4.43
Changes	2	2	2	3	2

CTS: Chicago Train Station, IL **MCT**: Michigan City, IN

164. Which train has the longest journey time?

(A) G56 (C) V344

(B) HJ89 (D) G211

165. To be in Michigan City by 2 p.m., which train should you take?

(A) G983 or HJ89 (C) V344

(B) G56 (D) any of them

166. What is a disadvantage to taking train HJ89?

(A) It has a longer journey time.

(B) You must change trains more often.

(C) It arrives earlier than train G983.

(D) It leaves earliest in the morning.

Question 167–169 refer to the following notice.

Young Roots in Photos and Film

Wednesday 17 Oct, 2.00–4.30 p.m.

Filmhouse and the *Heritage Lottery Fund* are proud to present *Young Roots in Photos and Film.* Over the last four years, young people across Scotland have run projects with money from the *Heritage Lottery Fund's* Young Roots grant scheme. This exhibition of photos and films showcases how young people have explored what remains important to them about their own heritage in the context of our dynamic modern world.

Cost: £5.00 per person. (Discounts available for professional artists and photographers.)

Call Beverley on 0131 623 8031 to book.

167. Where would this notice most likely be found?

(A) in a restaurant

(B) in a cinema

(C) in a lottery shop

(D) in an office

168. When could you see *Young Roots in Photos and Film?*

(A) one day only

(B) on certain days

(C) throughout the month of October

(D) over the last four years

169. What is the subject of the exhibition?

(A) young Scottish people

(B) the Heritage Lottery Fund

(C) a four-year exploration of Scotland

(D) how young people view their heritage

Questions 170–172 refer to the following text message chain.

Mark Richardson 10.20
Hi, Kim. How are things back at the office? The meeting went great here. We even got the chance to visit Kew Gardens in London.

Kim Swift 10.22
Don't worry about us, Mark. We're doing just fine. Tell me more about Kew Gardens.

Mark Richardson 10.24
We went on a tree identification tour for about one and a half hours. It was really cheap, too. We only paid £5, but this did not include entrance to the gardens. Anyway, we were lucky James had prebooked the tour, otherwise we wouldn't have been able to go on it.

Kim Swift 10.25
Well, that sounds amazing! How was the weather while you were there? Let me guess! It was raining, wasn't it?

Mark Richardson 10.29
It was for the most part, yes, but we had already been told to wear "suitable outdoor clothing and footwear" so I didn't mind.

Kim Swift 10.31
So tours are on in all but the most inclement weather, ha? Got to go now, Mark. Call me when you land.

Mark Richardson 10.32
I'll sure do. Good luck with the Stevens contract tomorrow.

170. How much should you expect to pay as a group if you are going on the tour?
(A) less than £5 (B) £5 exactly
(C) more than £5 (D) no more than £15

171. What should you do if you want to take the tour?
(A) enter the gardens as well
(B) book a place in advance
(C) go only on a sunny day
(D) buy special equipment

172. At 10.25, why does Kim write, "Let me guess!"?
(A) She expects London to be rainy.
(B) She is certain that the weather was nice.
(C) She doesn't want the man to tell her about the weather.
(D) She already knows what the weather was like.

Questions 173–175 refer to the following email.

To:	**All Employees**
From:	**Management**
Subject:	**Vacations**

This is to provide notice to all ComCast employees of our new company policy in regards to vacations.

Until recently, personnel needed to let management know about their vacation plans only one week before their holiday started. From now on, notice of your intention to take a vacation must be given to the company no less than a month prior to your vacation. This will enable us to employ temporary help if necessary, and to schedule vacations in a manner that will not be disruptive to the company.

There is a form that you must fill out to provide notice, which you may pick up in the Personnel Office.

Thank you for your cooperation.
Bill Chambers
Personnel Department

173. What was the policy on vacations like before?
(A) Vacations were not allowed.
(B) More notice was required.
(C) Less notice was required.
(D) Vacations were scheduled by the company.

174. What is a reason the company gives for making the changes?
(A) to make the process fairer
(B) to have time to hire extra workers
(C) to save the company money
(D) to limit the choice of vacation times

175. How do you give notice of the vacation you wish to take?
(A) tell Bill Chambers
(B) post it on your office door
(C) fill out a form
(D) tell your manager

Questions 176–180 refer to the following leaflet and letter.

VICTORIA CONFERENCE CENTER

Share ideas, be inspired

In the heart of downtown Victoria, British Columbia, by the spectacular Inner Harbor, is the Victoria Conference Center, a bright, modern, and technically advanced meeting place that is most inviting.

The average size of the conferences we host is 450–1,000 delegates. However, we have hosted groups as large as 2,500 delegates. Since conferences have distinct design and function space requirements, defining a maximum size is truly dependent on the event. We work to make the space fit your conference program. We are creative thinkers and enjoy working closely with clients to fashion the perfect venue.

May 18

Mary Ann Fisher
34 Australia Street
Bristol, UK

Dear Ms. Fisher,

Thank you for your inquiry about our company,Tourism Victoria. I am delighted to hear you have chosen our city to host your conference. Let me tell you a little about what our company can offer you.

We can plan special events, entertainment, and excursions, such as eco-adventures, symphony concerts, and tours for your delegates. We'll be happy to provide you with information on how to arrange pre- and post-event activities to suit your needs.

Tourism Victoria can also assist in promoting your organization's conference to stimulate delegate attendance with brochures and lure pieces. We'll act as liaison between our 900-plus member businesses and your planning committee.

I have enclosed an information leaflet on the Victoria Conference Center, which I highly recommend as a venue for your conference.

Please contact me if you have any questions.

Sincerely,

Bob Whitehall
Marketing
Tourism Victoria, Canada

176. What is the purpose of the leaflet?
(A) to educate people
(B) to promote something
(C) to invite people to an event
(D) to offer a discount

177. What is true of the letter?
(A) It was unsolicited.
(B) It answers an inquiry.
(C) It follows a purchase.
(D) It requests a service.

178. What has been decided for sure by Ms Fisher?
(A) She will work with Tourism Victoria.
(B) She will have a conference in the city of Victoria.
(C) She will hold the conference at the Victoria Conference Center.
(D) She will arrange an eco-adventure.

179. Where is the Victoria Conference Center located?
(A) in the downtown area
(B) near the downtown area
(C) by the sea, outside town
(D) 900 meters from the town

180. Where is Ms Fisher from?
(A) England
(B) Canada
(C) United States
(D) Australia

Practice Test 1

Questions 181–185 refer to the following letter and insert.

Occupier
Ravencroft Business Center
Portland, OR 34227

Dear Sir or Madam,

We are contacting you to inform you that, due to work on the electricity grid, your area will be without electricity for approximately four hours on the morning of September 12th. We hope that you understand that this maintenance is necessary, and we suggest that you read the insert on how to survive a power cut in order to minimize your inconvenience.

Sincerely,
William Tyler
Municipal Electricity

SURVIVING A POWER CUT

How you should prepare:

- Have a battery-powered radio tuned into a news station to receive updates.
- Keep a supply of candles, but don't leave candles or heaters unattended. Place them where you won't knock them over. A flashlight may be a safer alternative; keep the batteries renewed.

If power is interrupted:

- Switch off and unplug sensitive electronic appliances, such as personal computers, video players, satellite receivers, answering machines, etc.
- Don't open freezers and fridges more than absolutely necessary.
- Leave a light on so you know when the power has been restored.
- Check to see if your neighbors are OK.
- Keep a flask of hot drink near you.
- Wrap up warm.
- Keep one room warm and stay in it.

181. What is the purpose of the letter?
(A) to sell a product
(B) to make an apology
(C) to give a warning
(D) to make a request

182. What is true about the power cut?
(A) It is due to an accident.
(B) It is unknown how long it will last.
(C) It was planned in advance.
(D) It involves the whole city.

183. What may not be completely safe?
(A) a battery-powered radio
(B) leaving a light on
(C) a torch
(D) candles

184. What should NOT be turned on during a power cut?
(A) electric lights
(B) computers
(C) heaters
(D) the telephone

185. What is NOT recommended that you do during a powercut?
(A) help your neighbors
(B) defrost your fridge
(C) keep warm
(D) listen for updates

Questions 186–190 refer to the following email, attachment, and advert.

To:	Richard Brown
From:	Tara Larson
Subject:	Restaurant booking

Hi Richard,

I've found a promising-looking restaurant for our company lunch; it's *Bell's Diner*. I went yesterday with my cousin and her husband, and the food was really something.

It's not the typical diner you might think of! It has an informal, friendly atmosphere, sophisticated yet rustic decor, equally sophisticated modern European menu and rather elegant clientele. It is housed in a Victorian building split into two rooms, and I think one is available for group reservations, so that would be ideal.

Shall I go ahead and make a reservation? Lunch goes on rather late in the afternoon, as you can see from the information I've attached, so there shouldn't be any problem if the Design Department meetings run a little over time.

Tara Brown
Reception

Job vacancy

Sous chef–Full-time

Must be competent in vegetarian and vegan cuisine as this is our speciality.

Salary dependent on experience.

Please apply in writing to George Menes – Manager

Cuisine:	Modern European	
Times:	*Lunch* Tues–Sat *Dinner* Mon–Sat Closed Sundays	Midday–3 p.m. 7 p.m.–10.30 p.m.
Dress code:	None	
Payment:	All methods of payment accepted except Diners	
Av. price:	$24 and under	

186. How does Tara Larson know the restaurant is good?

(A) She knows from experience.

(B) A friend recommended it.

(C) She saw an advertisement.

(D) She was told by Mr Brown.

187. What did Tara Larson think of the food?

(A) She absolutely hated it.

(B) She didn't have an opinion about it.

(C) She thought it was OK.

(D) She liked it very much.

188. The people eating in the restaurant are described as

(A) Victorian.

(B) well-dressed.

(C) informally dressed.

(D) typical diner customers.

189. When can the company schedule their lunch?

(A) Monday at 11.30 a.m.

(B) Sunday at noon

(C) Wednesday at 2 p.m.

(D) Saturday at 7 p.m.

190. What is the restaurant famous for?

(A) children's parties

(B) catering for dietary needs

(C) its architecture

(D) its celebrity chefs

Questions 191–195 refer to the following notice, letter, and email.

Mr George Woodhouse
74 Meadow Lane
San Diego, CA 44613

Dear Mr Woodhouse,

Thank you for your interest in our course. Yes, there are still places available. You have two options: we have an intensive weekend course which runs for two weekends at the beginning of September, both Saturdays and Sundays, for eight hours each day, and we also have evening courses that meet from 7 – 9 p.m. on Tuesdays or Thursdays for three months. Both courses cost $900.

The courses are held at the Community College, and you would need to go there to register.

I would recommend you register as soon as possible as the courses are filling up quickly!

If you have further questions, you can call me at 376 334 4524 between 8 a.m. and 4 p.m.

Karen Miller
Admissions

Online Banking and Business Banking Course

How can you find the best online bank for you? Within the last decade, online banking has exploded in popularity and revolutionized the industry, but some banks offer better services than others.

In this course, we look at some things you should consider when you choose an online bank, including account access, security, online bill paying, account aggregation, and fees.

Learn how to use online banking to your advantage.

Hi Mary,

You know we were discussing how tricky we both find online banking? Well, not anymore! I've found a course we could both attend.

I'm out this morning till about 11.30 and I'm at the dentist's at 4, but I'm here before then, so give me a ring.

George

191. What does the course teach?
(A) how to start an online bank
(B) how to use online banking
(C) how to use the internet
(D) how to succeed as a banker

192. Why did Mr Woodhouse contact Karen Miller?
(A) to ask for information
(B) to answer a question
(C) to register for a course
(D) to set up a bank account

193. When could Mr Woodhouse take the course?
(A) Saturday evenings
(B) all day Tuesday
(C) Thursday evenings
(D) Tuesday mornings

194. What is true of the weekend courses?
(A) They are cheaper than the evening courses.
(B) They are full.
(C) They last for two hours per day.
(D) They last for four days.

195. Why does the man write, "Well, not anymore!"?
(A) He now knows how online banking works.
(B) He doesn't use online banking anymore.
(C) He no longer wants to discuss online banking with the woman.
(D) He has found a solution to their problem.

Questions 196–200 refer to the following email, leaflet, and text message chain.

To:	rogers@westways.com
From:	la_air@marriott.com
Subject:	Internet Access
Date:	June 12th

Dear Mr Rogers,

Thanks for your inquiry about staying with us. **-[1]-** We do have rooms available on the 24th and 25th.

-[2]- Regarding your question about availability of internet, we do have wireless internet access available in all public spaces in the hotel, for standard connection fees. **-[3]-** But let me recommend our Wired for Business Plan which offers you internet access in your room at great savings. **-[4]-** If we can be of any further assistance, please do not hesitate to contact us:

Los Angeles Airport Marriott
5855 West Century Boulevard
Los Angeles, California 90045, USA
Sales phone: 1-310-337-5331
Sales fax: 1-310-337-8084

WIRED FOR BUSINESS

Connecting you to the world!

For a set daily rate of 12.95 USD, you get, in your guest room:

1. High-speed internet access
2. Unlimited local phone calls
3. Unlimited long-distance calls (within the US)

This offer is good only in business suites.

John 11.44
Bob, you've stayed at the Marriott, before, haven't you?

Bob 11.45
Yes, when we had to meet those investors. Can't remember their names. Why?

John 11.47
I need you to pop into my office and give me the low-down on this hotel.

Bob 11.49
Sure. No problem. I'm downtown now, but I'll get back in less than an hour.

John 11.51
OK, because I've got a meeting with Parkers & Sons about the takeover bid in less than four hours.

196. Why was this email sent?
(A) to offer a service
(B) to answer an inquiry
(C) to recommend accommodation
(D) to acknowledge a booking

197. In which of the positions marked [1], [2], [3], and [4] does the following sentence best belong?
"I've attached a leaflet that gives you a bit more information about the plan."
(A) [1] (C) [3]
(B) [2] (D) [4]

198. If Mr Rogers does not use the Wired For Business Plan, where can he use the internet?
(A) in a public park (C) in his hotel room
(B) in the hotel lobby (D) at an internet cafe

199. What is most likely true about Mr Rogers?
(A) He has been to LA before on business.
(B) He is not sure where the hotel is.
(C) He has stayed at the Marriott before.
(D) He will be joined by his business partner later.

200. If you have purchased the Wired For Business Plan, what do you still have to pay extra for?
(A) wireless internet
(B) internet in your own room
(C) local phone calls
(D) international phone calls

Test 2

SECTION 1

Listening

In this section of the test, you will have the chance to show how well you understand spoken English. There are four parts to this section, with special directions for each part.

Part 1: Photographs

Directions: For each question, you will see a picture and you will hear four short statements. The statements will be spoken just one time. They will not be printed in your test book so you must listen carefully to understand what the speaker says. When you hear the four statements, look at the picture and choose the statement that best describes what you see in the picture. Choose the best answer (A), (B), (C), or (D).

EXAMPLE:

Now listen to the four statements. You will hear:

(A) He is on the phone.

(B) She is driving the car.

(C) She is typing on the computer.

(D) He is sitting next to her.

Statement (D) best describes what you see in the picture. Therefore, you should choose answer (D).

Sample Answer

A		B		C		D	✔

1. (A) ___ (B) ___ (C) ___ (D) ___

2. (A) ___ (B) ___ (C) ___ (D) ___

3. (A) ___ (B) ___ (C) ___ (D) ___

4. (A) ___ (B) ___ (C) ___ (D) ___

5

5. (A) ___ (B) ___ (C) ___ (D) ___

6

6. (A) ___ (B) ___ (C) ___ (D) ___

Part 2: Question–Response

Directions: In this part of the test, you will hear a question or statement spoken in English, followed by three responses, also spoken in English. The question or statement and the responses will be spoken just one time. They will not be printed in your test book, so you must listen carefully. You are to choose the best response to each question or statement. Now listen to a sample question.

You will hear: Man: Why are you late?
Woman: (A) I hope I won't be.
(B) My car broke down.
(C) He always is.

The best response is choice (B): "My car broke down". Therefore, you should choose (B).

7. (A) (B) (C)
8. (A) (B) (C)
9. (A) (B) (C)
10. (A) (B) (C)
11. (A) (B) (C)
12. (A) (B) (C)
13. (A) (B) (C)
14. (A) (B) (C)
15. (A) (B) (C)
16. (A) (B) (C)
17. (A) (B) (C)
18. (A) (B) (C)
19. (A) (B) (C)
20. (A) (B) (C)
21. (A) (B) (C)
22. (A) (B) (C)
23. (A) (B) (C)
24. (A) (B) (C)
25. (A) (B) (C)
26. (A) (B) (C)
27. (A) (B) (C)
28. (A) (B) (C)
29. (A) (B) (C)
30. (A) (B) (C)
31. (A) (B) (C)

Part 3: Conversations

Directions: You will hear some conversations between two or more people. You will be asked to answer three questions about what the speakers say in each conversation. Select the best response to each question and mark the letter (A), (B), (C), or (D) on your answer sheet. The conversations will not be printed in your test book and will be spoken only one time.

32. What is the reason for the traffic on 35E?

(A) an accident
(B) bad weather
(C) rush hour
(D) roadworks

33. What is the reason for the woman's nervousness?

(A) not knowing the material
(B) psychological obstacles
(C) pressure from other people
(D) her stutter

34. What, according to the man, is the most important part of the presentation?

(A) its substance
(B) its delivery
(C) its comprehensibility
(D) its flow

35. Why does the man want to find Meredith?

(A) to talk about their meeting tonight
(B) to prepare her on the Knight file
(C) to get a file he needs
(D) to make sure she is prepared for tonight

36. What is the man upset about?

(A) his tendency to postpone things
(B) Meredith's irresponsibility
(C) the content of the meeting
(D) Meredith's inability to help him

37. What does the man imply he will do at the meeting tonight?

(A) improvise
(B) ask to reschedule
(C) not attend
(D) lead the meeting

38. What effect did the interviewer have on the man?

(A) He made him feel arrogant.
(B) He encouraged him.
(C) He took advantage of him.
(D) He unnerved him.

39. What, besides the interview, could help the man get the job?

(A) his career goals
(B) his performance today
(C) his grades in school
(D) his motivation to be the best

40. What is the woman's opinion?

(A) The decision to hire him for the job depends on many factors.
(B) He should have shown that he is self-confident.
(C) The interviewer was nice but strict.
(D) His employment depends solely on the interviewer's opinion.

41. Where are the three individuals?
(A) their gate
(B) the security line
(C) the baggage claim area
(D) the convention center

42. Why does the woman say, "Plus, I'm falling asleep!"?
(A) to remind them she hasn't slept during the flight
(B) to justify wanting to go to the hotel straight away
(C) to add another reason why she needs coffee
(D) to ask them to move a bit faster

43. Why does he want to pay for the coffee?
(A) They paid last time.
(B) They drove him to the airport.
(C) They want to pay on the way back.
(D) It was the woman's idea.

44. Who referred the woman to Dr Evans?
(A) a coworker
(B) a doctor
(C) the man
(D) her psychologist

45. Why does the woman want to be Dr Evans's patient?
(A) She wants some herbs.
(B) She is inefficient at work.
(C) She can't sleep at night.
(D) She has a food disorder.

46. Look at the graphic. What is the woman's name?
(A) Mrs Davis (C) Mrs Wilson
(B) Ms Smith (D) Ms Brown

	Wed	Thu	Fri
12.00–12.30			Mrs Davis
13.00–14.00		Mrs Wilson	
14.00–14.30	Ms Smith		Ms Brown

47. According to the man, what is unique about the woman?
(A) She works 14 hours.
(B) She loves a long day at work.
(C) She leaves for work late.
(D) She likes her work.

48. What does going to the Calvin Klein meeting probably mean for the woman?
(A) a new client for her to work with
(B) a chance to work in a different department
(C) She could be promoted at some point.
(D) She could work for Calvin Klein.

49. Why did the boss order a lot of a particular design?
(A) She values the woman's opinion.
(B) The Calvin Klein reps suggested it.
(C) They are sampling a new clothing line.
(D) The woman designed it herself.

50. Why is it acceptable for Ed to leave at 3.30?
(A) He already put in a full day.
(B) He is allowed to work half-days when he wants.
(C) He is his own boss.
(D) His boss changed his schedule.

51. What does the woman admire about the man?
(A) his bravery in leaving work early
(B) how he puts family first
(C) his ability to wake up so early all the time
(D) his ability to succeed in various aspects of life

52. How does the man reassure the woman?
(A) He tells her his life is not for everyone.
(B) He recounts his past successes.
(C) He tells her it's possible to combine work and leisure.
(D) He says she could do it, too, if she really wanted to.

53. What has the man gotten used to?
(A) the stress of deadlines
(B) non-returned phone calls
(C) that the woman is often late
(D) unexpected obstacles in publishing

54. What does the publishing company want to meet with the woman about?
(A) a novel she wants to write
(B) publishing a collection of her columns
(C) her irresponsibility
(D) her missing their last scheduled meeting

55. Why does the woman say, "Are you serious?"?
(A) She needs to know that the man can be trusted.
(B) The man does not take his job seriously.
(C) The man has lied to her before.
(D) She can't believe how lucky she is.

56. Why does the man want to be in advertising?
(A) He is inventive and smart.
(B) He was fired from his last job.
(C) He knows he is passionate about it.
(D) It's comparable to accounting.

57. According to the woman, why should he get the job at the agency?
(A) to become creative
(B) to compare it with his old job
(C) to get experience
(D) to add passion to his life

58. Look at the graphic. Which job would the man be most interested in and suitable for?
(A) Advertising Agency Project Manager
(B) Social Media Manager
(C) Marketing Director – Seasonal
(D) Email Marketing & Advertising Intern

Job Title	Experience Level	Estimated Salary
Advertising Agency Project Manager	Entry	$32,000
Social Media Manager	Mid	$62,000
Marketing Director – Seasonal	Senior	$80,000
Email Marketing & Advertising Intern	Entry	–

59. What might hinder James's chance at the job?
(A) his qualifications
(B) an unfair boss
(C) not being related to his boss
(D) Paul being ruthless

60. What does the woman think about Paul?
(A) He is unqualified.
(B) He will try to persuade Cindy.
(C) He has an advantage.
(D) He is better than James.

61. What does the man know about Paul?
(A) his current emotional state
(B) that he is related to Cindy
(C) his level of disappointment
(D) that he already has the position

62. What is wrong with John?
(A) His report hasn't been printed.
(B) He didn't have time to write a report.
(C) There are no printers working in the office.
(D) He didn't get the promotion.

63. What does the woman think about the men's behavior?
(A) They are selfish.
(B) They are jealous.
(C) They are childish.
(D) They are dishonest.

64. What is the relationship between the man and the woman?
(A) boss and employee
(B) relatives
(C) neighbors
(D) coworkers

65. What is the man's job?
(A) architect
(B) accountant
(C) information technology expert
(D) builder

66. How can the man be described?
(A) cautious
(B) independent
(C) bored
(D) dishonest

67. How did the women feel about the man's behavior?
(A) impressed
(B) angry
(C) suspicious
(D) indifferent

68. What happened to the man?
(A) He nearly lost his job.
(B) His boss had an accident.
(C) He broke a machine at work.
(D) He had an accident at work.

69. What did the man do?
(A) apply for financial compensation
(B) buy a new car
(C) crash his company car
(D) pay money to his boss

70. What does the woman think the man should do?
(A) make a good impression at work
(B) forget about the money
(C) leave his job temporarily
(D) ask for more money

Part 4: Talks

Directions: You will hear some talks given by a single speaker. You will be asked to answer three questions about what the speaker says in each talk. Select the best response to each question and mark the letter (A), (B), (C), or (D) on your answer sheet. The talks will not be printed in your test book and will be spoken only one time.

71. What might flight cuts result in?
(A) the selling of the company
(B) lowered salaries
(C) being bought by another airline
(D) a higher ticket selling price

72. In what year might airlines have experienced the same problem?
(A) 1980 (C) 1989
(B) 1994 (D) never

73. What will airlines now make an effort to do?
(A) discourage business travelers
(B) reduce the number of seats they sell
(C) sell fewer cheap tickets via the internet
(D) sell more seats than usual

---

74. What kind of vehicle could be blocking the entryway?
(A) shuttle bus (C) car
(B) taxi (D) city bus

75. Where is the Ford Taurus allowed to be parked?
(A) west side parking lot
(B) off the premises
(C) a few meters away from where it is now
(D) south side parking lot

76. What will happen if it is not moved in 10 minutes?
(A) The police will be called.
(B) It will be removed by another vehicle.
(C) The owner will pay a fee.
(D) The entryway will continue to be blocked.

---

77. Besides variety, what else is heralded as being unique about shopping in New Hampshire?
(A) No tax is added to purchases.
(B) Nationally known name brands are sold.
(C) It specializes in sports equipment.
(D) All stores are old-fashioned.

78. What service do many stores provide?
(A) They help you find exactly what you are looking for.
(B) They will tell you the story behind your purchase.
(C) They gift-wrap your purchases for you.
(D) They will send purchases to you.

79. What tradition does New Hampshire uphold?
(A) telling oral stories about their past
(B) listing their stores by region
(C) making items that reflect and contain human spirit
(D) expanding their businesses from their home to workshops

---

80. Why are haircuts and car repairs mentioned?
(A) They are being promoted.
(B) They usually provide substandard service.
(C) They are examples of a service.
(D) They are being argued against.

81. When can reasonable timing of the service be expected?
(A) when a time has to be worked out
(B) in the less complicated services
(C) when the place providing the service is not busy
(D) in all cases

82. Why is a leaky roof mentioned?
(A) to illustrate unacceptable substandard service
(B) to demonstrate how often things go wrong in services
(C) to show that service will never be perfect
(D) to show that services often use low-quality materials

83. What is considered as food for our brain?

(A) oxygen

(B) cells

(C) blood

(D) the food we intake

84. When in the lungs, what does the blood give away?

(A) oxygen
(C) cells
(B) carbon dioxide
(D) air

85. What is the purpose of this text?

(A) to help patients improve their lives

(B) to inform doctors about blood diseases

(C) to help people understand their blood system

(D) to inform parents about children's blood diseases

---

86. When was the Registration of Business Names Act repealed?

(A) 1916
(C) 1982
(B) 1985
(D) never

87. What does the Business Names Act allow?

(A) complete freedom in choosing a name for your business

(B) for the government to have some say in your business's name

(C) the right to not tell others the name of your business

(D) the business to choose its name without government consultation

88. What is the main purpose of the mentioned rules?

(A) to maintain a variety of business names

(B) to ensure socially acceptable business names

(C) to keep the government involved in business life

(D) to protect people's ownership of names

---

89. What is NOT a mentioned event at the first modern Olympics?

(A) pole-vaulting
(C) soccer
(B) tennis
(D) gymnastics

90. What was Alfred Hoyos Guttmann's biggest difficulty?

(A) coming in first

(B) enduring the cold water

(C) maintaining a big lead

(D) swimming along with the current

91. How many individuals participated in the first modern Games?

(A) about 1,300
(C) exactly 300
(B) more than 3,000
(D) around 300

---

92. What time do they need to arrive at the airport?

(A) 07.30 sharp
(C) 06.00 sharp
(B) 06.30 a.m.
(D) around 06.00

93. Which is NOT a mentioned way they can entertain themselves on the plane?

(A) walking around
(C) reading a book
(B) having a snack
(D) taking a nap

94. Look at the graphic. Which one is their flight number?

(A) AO589
(C) CA693
(B) BE475
(D) PE125

Flight Number	Departure local time	From	To	Arrival local time: +7 hrs
AO589	07.30	New York, NY	Athens, Greece	21.00
BE475	06.00	Athens, Greece	New York, NY	08.00
CA693	07.30	New York, NY	Athens, Greece	23.30
PE125	07.30	Athens, Greece	New York, NY	09.30

95. How do we learn how to prepare for events such as pain?

(A) operant conditioning

(B) classical conditioning

(C) observational Learning

(D) modeling

96. What do we learn to avoid through operant conditioning?

(A) repetition

(B) excessive anticipation

(C) being mimicked

(D) unfavorable consequences

97. How are humans classified?

(A) as being in a higher group than animals

(B) as being non-imitative

(C) as a more sophisticated animal

(D) as immune to modeling

98. What is Janet's job?

(A) Mr Jones's assistant

(B) a nurse

(C) Mr Samuels' secretary

(D) a travel agent

99. Look at the graphic. When is the rescheduled meeting likely to take place?

(A) on Tuesday

(B) on Wednesday

(C) on Thursday

(D) on Friday

100. What does the woman mean when she says, "We are so sorry about the short notice."?

(A) They could have informed Mr Jones sooner.

(B) Something unexpected came up.

(C) Mr Samuels should have called himself.

(D) She forgot to call them as soon as she found out.

Mon	**10 a.m.**	*meeting at HQ*
Tue	**10 p.m.**	*fundraiser*
Wed	**1 p.m.**	*lunch w/Paul Fisher*
Thurs	**10 a.m.**	*dentist*
Fri	**9 p.m.**	*office party*

Vocabulary Development for Test 2, Reading, Parts 5 & 6

implication (n): a possible result

swift (adj): happening quickly

collective (adj): involving a group of people

adversity (n): an unpleasant situation

tribulation (n): a problem, a misfortune

solvent (adj): able to pay debts

compromise (n): a solution to a problem in which the people involved reduce their demands in order to agree

scorn (v): to show disrespect to someone or something

ambiguous (adj): having more than one meaning

ambidextrous: (adj) able to use both hands very well

breakthrough (n): an important event that improves a situation

burnout (n): the state of being mentally or physically tired because of overworking

rapport (n): a friendly relationship in which people understand each other well

redundant (adj): someone who lost their job because they are no longer needed

surplus (adj): more than needed

agitated (adj): nervous or restless

pivotal (adj): essential, very important

detrimental (adj): harmful

glide (v): to move easily, slide

soar (v): to rise quickly

uppermost (adj): more important than other things

cutback (n): a reduction in something

remit (v): to cancel or reduce a debt, a punishment, etc.

expenditure (n): amount of money spent

Vocabulary Development for Test 2, Reading, Parts 5 & 6

Exercise A

Choose the correct answer, (A), (B), or (C), to complete the sentences.

1. The new scheme has serious .... for the local economy.

   (A) compromises (C) expenditure

   (B) implications

2. In a .... between management and unions, a five per cent pay rise was agreed in return for an increase in productivity.

   (A) compromise (C) burnout

   (B) tribulation

3. They don't encourage people to keep .... funds in their current account.

   (A) swift (C) ambidextrous

   (B) surplus

4. House prices .... a further 25 per cent.

   (A) soared (C) glided

   (B) remitted

Exercise B

Choose the correct word, (A), (B), or (C), to fill the gaps in the text.

Miss Scott has excellent managerial skills and develops very good **(5)** .... with her staff. Today she is forced to announce the bad news to two employees. She needs to tell them that they will be made **(6)** .... because the company cannot afford to keep so many staff. The company managed to remain **(7)** .... during the recession, but now it is facing a lot of competition and it needs to survive.

5. (A) rapport (B) adversity (C) compromise
6. (A) surplus (B) uppermost (C) redundant
7. (A) ambiguous (B) agitated (C) solvent

Exercise C

Complete the sentences using the correct form of three of the words in the box below.

breakthrough	cutback	solvent	detrimental	ambiguous
scorn	burnout	collective	uppermost	agitated

8. The closure of the Scranton factory is the company's biggest single .... so far.
9. The privatization of the rail company could be seriously .... to the economy.
10. The wording of the agreement is ...., so it requires further explanation before it can be signed.

SECTION 2

Reading

In the Reading test, you will read a variety of texts and answer several different types of reading comprehension questions. The entire Reading test will last 75 minutes. There are three parts, and directions are given for each part. You are encouraged to answer as many questions as possible within the time allowed. You must mark your answers on the separate answer sheet. Do not write your answers in your test book.

Part 5: Incomplete Sentences

Directions: A word or phrase is missing in each of the sentences below. Four answer choices are given below each sentence. Select the best answer to complete the sentence. Then mark the letter (A), (B), (C), or (D) on your answer sheet.

Example: Her boss was talking to her ....
(A) angry (B) friendly (C) angrily (D) unfriendly Correct answer: (C)

101. If you want to have a successful interview, you must make a good ....

(A) impatience (C) impression
(B) implication (D) inspiration

102. Tim was always helpful and cheerful with customers; ...., he was declared employee of the month.

(A) nevertheless (C) however
(B) therefore (D) because

103. Lea did a .... job on the advertising campaign; she didn't miss a single detail.

(A) through (C) thorough
(B) swift (D) detailing

104. Maureen gave a talk when .... the conference last week.

(A) she attended
(B) was attending
(C) attended
(D) she had attended

105. You can pay by card over the phone, or we can issue you .... an invoice.

(A) of (C) for
(B) on (D) with

106. One of the main reasons people attend conferences is for the .... opportunities.

(A) greeting (C) networking
(B) partnering (D) programming

107. .... hard work is important, so is spending time with family and friends.

(A) Since (C) In spite
(B) Likewise (D) While

108. The .... opinion of the delegates was that the conference was a great success.

(A) collect (C) collective
(B) collected (D) collecting

109. Did you hear that Mr Richards proposed .... corporate strategy at the meeting yesterday?

(A) a whole new (C) wholly new
(B) a new all (D) a new wholly

110. In regard .... your inquiry, we have no vacancies at this time.

(A) about (C) with
(B) from (D) to

111. Trevor chose to be a lawyer because he likes the ....

(A) adversity (C) tribulation
(B) struggle (D) challenge

112. All parties were happy with the results of the meeting because it was a .... situation.

(A) win-win (C) win-lose
(B) no-win (D) lose-lose

113. A lot of insurance companies are under pressure to increase premiums to stay ………………… .

(A) solvent (C) insolvent
(B) soluble (D) insoluble

114. The goals of the two CEOs were different, so it was not easy for them to reach a(n) ………………… which they were both happy with.

(A) dialogue (C) negotiation
(B) compromise (D) obligation

115. I thought the new delegate ………………… here this afternoon. Where is she?

(A) is (C) would be
(B) was being (D) will be

116. After making some changes, both the ………………… and the profits of the company increased.

(A) productivity (C) producing
(B) producers (D) product

117. This factory has the ………………… to produce 10,000 smartphone devices per year.

(A) skill (C) capacity
(B) rate (D) pace

118. I ………………… to inform you that your application for the job has not been successful.

(A) scorn (C) regret
(B) hesitate (D) grieve

119. I would suggest you ………………… with Personnel before buying the plane ticket.

(A) have checked (C) checked
(B) checking (D) check

120. Leila is …………………; I know she will rise to the top quickly.

(A) ambitious (C) ambiguous
(B) advantageous (D) ambivalent

121. After ………………… worked as a senior executive for 20 years, Peter decided to retire.

(A) has had (C) having
(B) he was having (D) he has

122. Having worked for 10 years as an accountant, Tom was suffering from ……………… and decided to change careers.

(A) breakthrough (C) breakout
(B) burnout (D) blackout

123. The company is doing so well that the chairman was smiley and ………………… during the meeting.

(A) cheering (C) cheerful
(B) cheers (D) cheer up

124. It's not advisable to rent a commercial property in this area as the business ………………… will be very high.

(A) rapport (C) rates
(B) ranges (D) rumor

125. I specifically asked you ………………… here by 8 a.m.! What is your excuse this time?

(A) to be (C) are
(B) would be (D) being

126. The security guard was made ………………… when the bank installed a new high-tech alarm system.

(A) redundant (C) excessive
(B) surplus (D) retiree

127. Jennifer was one of only three candidates ……………… for an interview.

(A) offered (C) invited
(B) employed (D) hired

128. The first-aid seminar is ……………….; you must attend.

(A) obligated (C) obligatory
(B) obligation (D) obliging

129. Alexander is a superb architect, but his ………………… are rather high so we gave the job to someone else.

(A) salary (C) dues
(B) costs (D) fees

130. It was ………………… of Judy to quit her job – she'll probably be sorry later.

(A) rash (C) handy
(B) negligent (D) inconsiderate

Part 6: Text Completion

Directions: Read the texts that follow. A word or phrase is missing in some of the sentences. Four answer choices are given below each of the sentences. Select the best answer to complete the text. Then mark the letter (A), (B), (C), or (D) on your answer sheet.

Questions 131–134 refer to the following letter.

Fly Away Airlines
Newforth Business Park
Minneapolis, MN 27726

Dear Sir or Madam,

I am sending this letter of .... because of the service I received while traveling on your Flight 779 from Minneapolis to New York on September 19th.

131. (A) complain (C) complaint
(B) complains (D) complaining

I requested a diabetic meal through your website and confirmed this when I checked in for the flight. However, when the meals were served on board, I was told that there was no diabetic meal requested. I had to ask four times and become quite .... before the cabin crew would search for the meal which I had reason to believe was there. Mistakes may happen, but this seemed like unnecessary rudeness.

132. (A) complicated (C) interrogated
(B) motivated (D) agitated

You can understand my concern, I'm sure, because eating regular meals, made up of the right foods, is .... in managing this illness. ....

Sincerely,
John Baker

133. (A) critical (C) trivial
(B) creative (D) valuable

134. (A) To sum up, I was greatly satisfied with your service.
(B) Luckily, the chef offered to make me a diabetic meal on the spot.
(C) Regrettably, I'm not sure I would feel confident traveling with you in the future.
(D) To tell you the truth, I was disappointed in the meal's taste.

Questions 135–138 refer to the following news article.

More than $160m will be spent on music and video downloads in the USA this year, according to a ....

135. (A) fortune (C) poll
(B) summary (D) critic

Market analysts predict that digital downloads will be worth $193m next year, up 45.5% on last year. And digital spending will continue to ...., reaching $700m a year by the end of the decade, according to USA Music and Video Streaming's latest report.

136. (A) sink (C) glide
(B) float (D) soar

But CD and DVD spending has slowed, with the .... USA music and video market down 2.9%, to $4bn this year.

137. (A) altogether (C) overall
(B) whole (D) absolute

.........................., sales of vinyl have increased as records make a spectacular resurgence.

138. (A) Instead
(B) Due to this
(C) On the other hand
(D) Whatsoever

Questions 139–142 refer to the following memo.

MEMO

To: All Staff
From: Management
Date: April 4th

.... I would like to remind you of how important it is to avoid any problems with the health inspection. It is essential that you carry .... your usual cleaning and sanitation procedures with the utmost care this week. Do not take ....

139. (A) This is to inform you about a change of plans.
(B) Thank you for your cooperation last week.
(C) As you know, we are expecting a visit from health inspectors this week.
(D) In light of recent events, all preparations are canceled.

140. (A) over (C) away
(B) off (D) out

141. (A) cutbacks (C) cut-offs
(B) short cuts (D) downturns

I would particularly like to remind staff to check on the storage of meat products. Make .... meats are kept on the upper shelf in the refrigeration unit, because the temperature is not high enough on the lower shelf.

Thank you for your cooperation.
Lisa Thomson
Management

142. (A) sure (C) obvious
(B) clear (D) careful

Questions 143–146 refer to the following email.

To: [Mark Ackerman] aker@globalnet.com
From: [Deborah Leach] leachd@abc.co
Subject: PARKING LOT REFURBISHMENT
Cc: [Summers] summc@abc.co
[Erin Young] youne@abc.co
Date: June 2, 14.12.

Dear Mr Ackerman,
This is to inform you that we have carefully .... your estimate for the parking lot refurbishing. We are planning to contract with you for this work.

143. (A) recalled (C) renewed
(B) reviewed (D) remitted

We are unable to sign this contract immediately, ..., as final approval of expenditures of this nature must come from the head office in New York.

144. (A) however (C) although
(B) despite (D) because

We expect to receive approval or disapproval .... the next 30 days. We will contact you with instructions accordingly.

145. (A) on (C) since
(B) within (D) among

If we may be of any assistance in the meantime, please feel free .... this office.

Sincerely,
Deborah Leach, Secretary
ABC Stationers
Denver, Colorado
Tel: 605 885 5624

146. (A) when you contact with
(B) contacting
(C) to contact
(D) to contact with

Vocabulary Development for Test 2, Reading, Part 7

spectacular (adj): great, very exciting to look at

undertake (v): to do something or to begin to do something, especially something difficult or something that will take a long time

representative: (adj) typical of, or the same as others in a group

sitting (adj): existing at the present time

refurbishment (n): work related to repairing, painting, and cleaning a building

commotion (n): a short period of noise, excitement, and confusion

clash (n): an argument

aisle (n): a narrow space between rows of seats or shelves, for example in an aircraft, cinema, or supermarket

syllabus (n): a study plan that shows which subjects will be studied on a particular course

manipulation (n): controlling someone or something to your own advantage, usually in an unfair way

stumble upon: (phr. v) to discover something

structured (adj): well-organized, with all the parts connected together

delegate (n): a person chosen to attend and/or speak for a group at a meeting

sustain (v): to experience or suffer (usually something bad or unpleasant)

discretion (n): the ability to decide something

intermittent (adj): stopping and starting repeatedly

obliged (adj): to be forced to do something because it's your duty

premises (n pl): an area owned by someone, especially an organization

enclose (v): to send something in the same letter or parcel

relieved (adj): happy that something unpleasant did not happen

Vocabulary Development for Test 2, Reading, Part 7

Exercise A

Choose the correct answer, (A), (B), or (C), to complete the sentences.

1. Please enclose your .... with your application.

(A) syllabus

(B) discretion

(C) resume

2. The company is relocating to new .... next month.

(A) premises

(B) manipulation

(C) refurbishment

3. There were violent .... between the police and demonstrators in the city center yesterday.

(A) commotions

(B) delegates

(C) clashes

4. The four-month course provides hands-on experience within a(n) .... program of study.

(A) structured

(B) representative

(C) obliged

Exercise B

Choose the correct word, (A), (B), or (C), to fill the gaps in the text.

I was doing my weekly shopping in my local supermarket. I was standing in the international food **(5)** .... , trying to find an Indian sauce for my curry, when I suddenly heard a lot of noise. I turned round to see what all the **(6)** .... was about. To my surprise, I saw one security guard chasing a man. 'He must be a shoplifter,' I thought. Then, to my horror, the man started running towards me, and it looked like he was going to hit me. I put my trolley in front of him, and he fell down. Then, in seconds, he was arrested, so I felt **(7)** ....

5.	(A) aisle	(B) premises	(C) commotion
6.	(A) premises	(B) discretion	(C) commotion
7.	(A) relieved	(B) obliged	(C) spectacular

Exercise C

Complete the sentences using the correct form of three of the words in the box below.

enclose	undertake	representative	sitting	manipulation
sustain	stumble upon	intermittent	discretion	syllabus

8. The head office building .... only minimal damage in the earthquake.

9. I don't think his views are .... of all the workers here.

10. Workers can be fired at the .... of the manager in this place.

Part 7: Reading Comprehension

Directions: You will read a selection of texts, such as magazine and newspaper articles, letters, and advertisements. Each text is followed by several questions. Select the best answer for each question and mark the letter (A), (B), (C), or (D) on your answer sheet.

Example: Are you someone who enjoys trying new things and does not feel uncomfortable in new environments? Then why not get paid for it? *CULTURE* magazine is looking for individuals to go to new clubs, events, etc., and write about the cultural scene they observe in these places. Interested? Send your resume to CULTURE@hotmail.com. Please, no phone calls.

What type of person would be best qualified for this job?

(A) a homebird (B) an introvert (C) a clumsy person (D) a risk-taker Correct answer: (D)

Questions 147–149 refer to the following advertisement.

Anthony's Pier

The world-famous Anthony's Pier has become synonymous with fine seafood, tasty American dishes, and spectacular views of the harbor and the city skyline. Established by Anthony Athanas in 1963, Anthony's Pier is one of four in the family of Athanas restaurants. A trolley service is provided for dinner customers heading off to the Fleet Boston Pavilion Concerts.

Full bar available and private dining room for corporate functions. Reservations recommended.

140 Northern Avenue, Boston, MA 02210
Phone: 617-482-6262 - Fax: 617-426-2324 - http://www.pier4.com

OPEN: Sunday 12 p.m.–10 p.m. (Dinner All Day)

Monday–Thursday 11:30 a.m.–10:00 p.m.
Friday and Saturday 11:30 a.m.–11:00 p.m.

Dress code is smart casual.

147. For what reason would you visit Anthony's Pier?

(A) to eat
(B) to fish
(C) for a stroll
(D) to see a concert

148. In which way can you NOT contact the restaurant?

(A) telephone
(B) letter
(C) email
(D) fax

149. What is unique about Sundays at Anthony's Pier?

(A) It is not open early in the morning.
(B) You can eat dinner at any time.
(C) It stays open late.
(D) There is a dress code.

Questions 150–151 refer to the following notice.

FLORIDA STATE UNIVERSITY
CAREER SERVICES

Join us at **CAREER EXPO**, to be held on Wednesday October 2 between the hours of 10 a.m. and 7 p.m. at the Holiday Inn Select, 3535 Ulmerton Road, Clearwater, Florida 33762.

For more information, contact Cheryl Thomson in the Careers Office – Tel: 286 331 3476

150. Where would this notice most likely be found?
(A) in a tourist office
(B) in a hotel lobby
(C) on a college campus
(D) in a newspaper

151. What is located on Ulmerton Road?
(A) Holiday Inn Select
(B) Florida State University
(C) the Careers Office
(D) Clearwater

Questions 152–154 refer to the following job announcement.

Organization:	UNESCO
Job type:	Science and Technology
Job reference:	EU/TP/ITA/SC/0822
Apply:	Click here
Job description:	Research Scientist
City:	Trieste
Country:	ITALY

Responsibilities

Research: To undertake front-line research in the area of mathematics; specifically, probability (pure and/or applied) and dynamical systems.

Qualifications

Education:
Ph.D. or equivalent doctoral level in mathematics.
Experience:
At least five years of research experience at an international level after completion of Ph.D.
Languages:
Excellent knowledge of written and spoken English.
Others:
A positive attitude towards the international and multicultural characteristics of the assignment.

152. Where is this job announcement most likely to be found?
(A) on a job center bulletin board
(B) in a newspaper
(C) on the internet
(D) in a magazine

153. What is true for the successful candidate?
(A) He or she must be Italian.
(B) He or she must be English.
(C) He or she must speak English.
(D) He or she should have just graduated with a Ph.D.

154. What will the research be about, specifically?
(A) probability
(B) international mathematics
(C) attitudes to multiculturalism
(D) a mathematician

Questions 155–157 refer to the following insert.

PHYSICAL DEMANDS

The physical demands described here are representative of those that must be met by an employee to successfully perform the essential functions of this job. Reasonable accommodation may be made to enable individuals with disabilities to perform the essential functions.

While performing the duties of this job, the employee is regularly required to actively listen to and communicate with supervisors, peers, and customers.

The employee must be capable of sitting and driving for extended periods of time depending on the geographic size of the service area.

The employee will consistently be required to work from high places such as roofs, ceilings, and ladders as well as from crawl spaces and other limited spaces within and outside of homes and businesses.

The employee must be able to safely move and lift materials and equipment weighing up to 25 pounds on a routine basis, and on limited occasions up to 50 pounds, without assistance.

155. Where would this insert most likely be found?

(A) in an office safety document

(B) in a staff newsletter

(C) at a health center

(D) in a job application pack

156. Who would not be able to perform this job well?

(A) anyone who is not a weightlifter

(B) someone who is afraid of heights

(C) someone with any kind of disability

(D) someone who reads slowly

157. What kind of job is being described?

(A) repair or maintenance work

(B) door-to-door sales work

(C) research or product development

(D) office work

Questions 158–160 refer to the following news article.

NEWS

Following some important business meetings, the President is due to meet the renowned Buddhist leader, despite strong objections from several sources. It will be the first time a sitting president will have appeared in public with the 72-year-old religious leader.

On Wednesday, the President will attend a ceremony at the Capitol, where the Buddhist leader will receive a Congressional Gold Medal, the top US civilian award.

A spokesman for the objectors said they would like the US "to correct the mistakes and to cancel the arrangements". A White House spokeswoman said that the President understood the concerns that had been expressed, but "we would hope that the objectors would get to know the religious leader as the President sees him – as a spiritual leader and someone who wants peace", she said.

158. What is unique about the meeting?

(A) A president has never appeared in public with the religious leader before.

(B) It is occurring in order to give the political leader a very prestigious award.

(C) It is supporting a new religious movement.

(D) It is the first time the religious leader has visited the US capital.

159. What is true about the religious leader?

(A) He is an important political influence in the US.

(B) He is in his seventies.

(C) He was an enemy of the US in the past.

(D) He is respected by everyone.

160. What does the President hope the objectors will do?

(A) protest

(B) stand up for their rights

(C) convert to Buddhism

(D) be more open-minded

Questions 161–163 refer to the following notice.

ATTENTION

The restrooms on Level 4 will be closed from 3 p.m. on Friday until 1 p.m. on Monday for refurbishment and replacement of the toilets. At this time, please use the restrooms on Level 1 or Level 2. Disabled toilets are available on Level 1.

During this time, there may also be extra activity and noise on Level 4. We apologize to those with offices on Level 4 for any inconvenience and appreciate your patience while we carry out this important work.

Management

161. Who is this notice meant for?

(A) office workers

(B) construction workers

(C) cleaners

(D) management

162. What will be true about the toilets on Tuesday?

(A) They will be being worked on.

(B) They will be in a new place.

(C) They will be new.

(D) They will be broken.

163. What is NOT an inconvenience that can be expected?

(A) a lack of toilet facilities

(B) extra noise

(C) extra commotion

(D) having to go further to reach a toilet

Questions 164–166 refer to the following receipt.

{Receipt for Finance Department}

1	Mushroom Risotto	$7.95
2	Chicken Salad	$6.00
1	Meat Lasagne	$8.95
1	Pepperoni Pizza	$8.88
2	Sparkling Water	$1.10
1	Orange Juice	$0.50
3	Chocolate Cake	$2.34

May 24, 1:30 p.m.

Total	$35.72
Tax @ 8%	$ 2.86
Grand Total	$38.58

Thank you and come again!

***This receipt entitles you to free parking if you present it at the payment kiosk on leaving.**

164. Which meal of the day is this receipt for?

(A) breakfast

(B) lunch

(C) dinner

(D) late-night snack

165. How many people probably ate?

(A) one

(B) two

(C) three

(D) four

166. What is not included in the bill?

(A) drinks

(B) sales tax

(C) desserts

(D) a tip

Questions 167–168 refer to the following news report.

Note for {**Mr Downing**}: **Shall we send this article to print for tomorrow's edition?**

Republicans Clash Over Tax Cuts

Republican party presidential candidates Mr Kiuliani and Mr Somney argued over their tax and spending policies. The clashes took place during a televised debate in New Mexico.

The ex-Austin, TX, mayor and the former Florida governor each claimed to be more committed to lowering taxes, as they competed for conservative support.

The clash between Mr Kiuliani and Mr Somney began when the Republican front-runners were asked to discuss their differences over economic issues.

167. What was Mr Kiuliani's former job?

(A) president

(B) mayor of Austin

(C) governor of Florida

(D) Republican presidential candidate

168. Where did most people probably witness the clash?

(A) on TV

(B) in New Mexico

(C) in Florida

(D) in Austin, TX

Questions 169–172 refer to the following email.

To:	"Anna Ardy" <a.ardy@rg_inc.org>
From:	"Mark Wilson" <m.wilson@rg_inc.org>
CC:	"Jason Johnson" <j.johnson@rg_inc.org>, "Bill Stewart" <Stewa78@gbv.gov>, "Maria White" <m.white@rg_inc.org>, "Jodie Forest" <j.forest@rg_inc.org>
Date:	PR committee meeting – Thursday November 12th
Attachments:	Monday November 8th 09.04

Just a reminder to everyone that we are holding our Public Relations Committee meeting this Thursday.

It is due to start at 9:00 sharp, with Mr Stewart kindly visiting to give a presentation on the new advertising regulations that have just passed, so this should save all of us some time and confusion. Also, would those of you who have had projects finished this month please be prepared to give a quick presentation on the outcome.

Thanks, and I look forward to seeing you at the meeting.

Mark Wilson

169. How many people received this email?

(A) one
(B) five
(C) eight
(D) nine

170. What is true of the meeting?

(A) It will start promptly.
(B) People will present ideas for projects.
(C) There will be several guest speakers.
(D) It is in a week's time.

171. What is most likely to be the website address of this organization?

(A) www.wilson.org
(B) www.gbv.gov
(C) www.rg_inc.gov
(D) www.rg_inc.org

172. What is the purpose of the meeting?

(A) to see who can give the best presentation
(B) to welcome a new employee
(C) to finish some projects
(D) to be informed about new rules

Questions 173–175 refer to the following card.

In case of an emergency landing, always follow the instructions of the crew. Aisle lights will guide you to the nearest exit, which may be located either in front of you or behind you. Please leave personal belongings behind and remove high-heeled shoes before using the inflatable exit slide. Do not inflate your life vest until after you have exited.

173. Where is this card most likely to be located?

(A) on a bus
(B) on a train
(C) on a ferry
(D) on a plane

174. How can you find the exit?

(A) by following the lights
(B) by looking in front and behind
(C) by asking the crew
(D) by reading the card

175. What should you take with you in an emergency landing?

(A) bags
(B) a life vest
(C) high-heeled shoes
(D) an inflatable slide

Questions 176–180 refer to the following web page and email.

SXHTML COURSE by IT SOLUTIONS

SXHTML is the next version of SHTML. **-[1]-** This class will teach all the same concepts as the SHTML 101 course, but will be focused on valid and well-formed SXHTML. After you finish this free 11-week course, you will understand the basics of SXHTML and some more advanced topics. **-[2]-** With interactive lessons and the option to work with other people on the course, you'll be able to learn SXHTML the way you want. **-[3]-**

The class will cover:

* the differences between SXHTML and SHTML

* an overview of forms * text manipulation

* basic SXHTML * lists, images, tables, and frames

At the end of the class, those students who pass a skills test demonstrating their knowledge will receive a certificate marking their successful completion of the course. -[4]-

To:	Josephine
From:	Alistair

Hi Josephine,
I just stumbled upon this website, and I thought of you because of our conversation last week, when you said your boss wants you to make a website for the business but you had no idea what to do. This course sounds perfect – and it's free, too! Actually, I remember my friend Tom did this course a while back and was very happy with it. The only thing he mentioned was that you can't change your email address for the whole 11 weeks of the course or you might have problems!

I hope it's useful for you!
Keep in touch,
Alistair

176. What is true of the course?
(A) It is the first course offered by IT Solutions.
(B) It is highly structured.
(C) You must know SHTML first.
(D) It has flexible options.

177. What is NOT taught in the course?
(A) how to use images
(B) what is new about SXHTML
(C) how texts can be manipulated
(D) details about every form

178. In which of the positions marked [1], [2], [3], and [4] does the following sentence best belong? "Go at your own pace, or follow along with the weekly syllabus."?
(A) [1] (C) [3]
(B) [2] (D) [4]

179. Where did Alistair find the information on the course?
(A) on the internet (C) his friend told him
(B) in a magazine (D) in a newspaper

180. What is the most likely relationship between Alistair and Josephine?
(A) colleagues (C) boss/employee
(B) friends (D) teacher/student

Questions 181–185 refer to the following email and attachment.

To:	**Terry Morrison**
From:	**Mabel Johansson, Events Coordinator**
Date:	**October 17, 13.05**
Attachments:	**MOBILE TECHNOLOGY CONFERENCE**

Hello Terry,

I was very relieved to hear that you will be available to help with registration activities at the conference. We were in a bit of a panic!

We need someone for Monday and Tuesday, just to sit at the registration desk and answer questions; you will also pass out the orientation packets to the delegates as they arrive. I've attached the schedule for the relevant days so you can have a look at the times.

Do let me know that you've received this email and the times are all right for you.

Thanks ever so much!

Regards,
Mabel

MOBILE TECHNOLOGY CONFERENCE

Early Registration	Monday, October 22	7.30 a.m.–5.00 p.m.
DAY ONE	Tuesday, October 23	
Registration Hours		8.00 a.m.–10.00 a.m.
Morning Technical Sessions		10.15 a.m.–12.00 p.m.
Lunch		12.00 p.m.–1.00 p.m.
Keynote Plenary Session		1.00 p.m.–3.00 p.m.
Exhibit Hall Open		2.00 p.m.–5.00 p.m.
Afternoon Technical Sessions		4.30 p.m.–7.00 p.m.

181. What will be included in Terry's job?
(A) organizing the conference
(B) giving delegates information
(C) leading a Technical Session
(D) answering the telephone

182. What would Mabel like Terry to do?
(A) let her know when there is a problem
(B) let her know that all is OK
(C) tell her what hours he is available
(D) volunteer to work

183. When will Terry be working on Tuesday?
(A) 8 a.m.–10 a.m.
(B) 8 a.m.–7 p.m.
(C) 7.30 a.m.–5 p.m.
(D) 7.30 a.m.–10 p.m.

184. Which conference activities are happening at overlapping times?
(A) the Exhibit Hall and the Afternoon Technical Sessions
(B) the Keynote Plenary Session and the Afternoon Technical Sessions
(C) Registration and the Morning Technical Sessions
(D) Lunch and the Keynote Plenary Session

185. How long are the Morning Technical Sessions?
(A) 2 hours
(B) 2 hours and 30 minutes
(C) 45 minutes
(D) 1 hour and 45 minutes

Questions 186–190 refer to the following letter, instant message chain and business card.

Mr Timothy York
42 Chadwick Street, Flat 6
Portland, OR 97207
January 18

We have received your claim for damages to your company car sustained on December 29. -[1]- We need a police report to determine fault in accident claims and request that you send us this document. -[2]- Were police present at the accident scene? If police were not involved, we will need a form 77RH from you.

In this situation, the claim process becomes more complicated, and it is at our discretion whether we can accept your claim. -[3]-

I am the officer at DriveRight Insurance who will be handling your claim, and I have included my business card with contact details. -[4]-

If you have any questions or need a copy of the 77RH form, please contact me directly.

Regards,
Mr Tyler Bancroft

Tim 8.10
Kylie, do you have the police report from my accident?

Kylie 8.12
Of course I do. What do you want it for?

Tim 8.14
I got a letter from DriveRight and they asked for it.

Kylie 8.16
OK, do you want me to bring it over to your desk?

Tim 8.17
No time! Send an email copy straight away to Bancroft@DriveRight.co.uk.

Mr Tyler Bancroft, MA
Claims Appraiser
DriveRight Insurance Co.
Mob: 778 4446 6925
Tel: 020 7429 8759
Fax: 020 7429 8755
email: Bancroft@DriveRight.co.uk

186. Approximately how much time has passed between the accident and this letter?
(A) a few days
(B) a few weeks
(C) a few months
(D) about a year

187. Why is a police report needed?
(A) to prove the accident happened
(B) to show who caused the accident
(C) to complete the 77RH form
(D) to show where the accident happened

188. In which of the positions marked [1], [2], [3], and [4] does the following sentence best belong? "However, we require a few other pieces of documentation to process the claim."
(A) [1]
(B) [2]
(C) [3]
(D) [4]

189. At 8.17, what does the man mean when he writes, "No time!"?
(A) He can't be at his office so fast.
(B) He can't talk to the woman now.
(C) It's time he said no to the woman.
(D) The situation calls for swift action.

190. In which department at DriveRight Insurance does Mr Bancroft most likely work?
(A) Management
(B) Sales Department
(C) Claims Department
(D) Police Department

Questions 191–195 refer to the following bulletin, memo, and email.

DEPARTMENTAL EMERGENCY ALARMS

IN THE EVENT OF AN ACCIDENT OR EMERGENCY WITHIN THE DEPARTMENT, THERE ARE THREE ALARMS THAT MAY BE HEARD: **KLAXON HORN**, **CONTINUOUS BELL,** OR **INTERMITTENT BELL.**

1) A KLAXON HORN INDICATES THAT A LABORATORY ALARM HAS BEEN ACTIVATED
- ☛ Trained staff will respond to this alarm during normal working hours.
- ☛ If this alarm should sound outside of normal working hours or persist for any period, you are obliged to investigate its cause.

2) A CONTINUOUSLY SOUNDING FIRE BELL
- ☛ In normal working hours, all staff are expected to follow the emergency procedures detailed in the safety regulations.

3) A LIFT ALARM INTERMITTENT BELL
- ☛ Local to the lift only. In normal working hours, inform the General Office on Level 4 of Building J13.
- ☛ If after normal working hours, inform Security on 13333.

MEMORANDUM

To: All Employees
From: Management

Following on from the uncertainty we experienced last week over procedures to follow when an alarm is heard, the attached document outlines the different alarms and the actions that need to be taken when they are sounded.

Please make yourself familiar with it.

Remember, however:
BEFORE YOU INVESTIGATE THE SOURCE OF ANY PROBLEM, RING and INFORM SECURITY – Phone No. 13333.
Give them the following information:
YOUR NAME
THE TYPE OF ALARM
THE ACTION YOU INTEND TO TAKE

To:	**All departments**
Subject:	**Alarms**

Just to add to the memo sent out earlier.

The alarms will be tested on a weekly basis, one after the other, in the following order:
- **laboratory**
- **fire**
- **lift**

This will happen at 9 a.m. every Monday morning.

Staff do not need to evacuate the building.

191. Which alarm is the least serious?
(A) the klaxon horn
(B) the continuously sounding bell
(C) the intermittent bell
(D) They are all equally serious.

192. When will the klaxon horn sound?
(A) if there is an emergency in the laboratory
(B) if there is a fire outside of working hours
(C) if someone is stuck in the lift
(D) if there is a fire at any time

193. For what reason do employees need to check the safety regulations?
(A) to learn the fire emergency procedures
(B) to learn how to avoid laboratory emergencies
(C) to learn emergency procedures outside of working hours
(D) to find out how to contact security

194. Why was the memo issued?
(A) as a routine safety precaution
(B) in answer to a question by staff
(C) because of an incident last week
(D) because the alarm system is new

195. What is said about alarm testing?
(A) It could happen at any time.
(B) It will happen twice a month.
(C) The fire alarm will go off first.
(D) It will be a regular procedure.

Questions 196–200 refer to the following letter, text message chain, and coupon.

BORDERING BOOKS

23 Pine Avenue
Ventura, CA 94553
April 25

Dear Neighbor,

A new store is opening near you! On Monday August 4th, doors are opening on our new Pine Avenue Branch of Bordering Books.

Our premises are spacious and light to make your shopping experience pleasant and, of course, we offer our signature Bordering Cafe coffee shop on the second floor, so you can sit with a coffee or tea while looking over potential purchases.

And, of course, as you've come to expect from Bordering Books, we have the largest selection of books around, including our new Business Books Section.

Because you are a neighbor, we are enclosing a special coupon to encourage you to come and get to know us.

Regards,
The Bordering Books Team

Come and meet us at Bordering Books!

This coupon is good for one hot drink and one pastry at the Pine Avenue Branch of Bordering Bookshop.

Valid until May 25th

Jim 13.24
Hi Bob, fancy going for a coffee at the new Bordering bookshop after work?

Bob 13.25
Coffee at a bookshop, eh? You're such a bookworm! But what are you after this time?

Jim 13.27
Is it that obvious? Ha ha ... I actually need to buy some books for my new physics course.

Bob 13.29
No problem, Jim. I could also look for this Spanish textbook I was telling you about.

Jim 13.31
Deal! I'll call you later.

196. How can Bordering Books best be described?
(A) a local business
(B) a chain of stores
(C) a multinational corporation
(D) a new business venture

197. Where does the person who received the letter probably live?
(A) on or near Pine Avenue
(B) anywhere in Ventura
(C) anywhere in California
(D) anywhere near a Bordering Books branch

198. What is Bordering Books known for?
(A) the Bordering Cafe coffee shops
(B) the low prices of the books they have
(C) the architecture of their shops
(D) their generous promotional activities

199. At 13.25, what does the man imply when he writes, "But what are you after this time?"?
(A) Jim often shops for books.
(B) Bob has reason to believe that Jim is hiding something.
(C) Jim always has an ulterior motive.
(D) Bob doesn't like being taken advantage of.

200. What can you get with the coupon?
(A) hot drinks for you and a friend
(B) a meal on August 4th
(C) a tea and a pastry
(D) a coffee and a book

Test 3

SECTION 1

Listening

In this section of the test, you will have the chance to show how well you understand spoken English. There are four parts to this section, with special directions for each part.

Part 1: Photographs

Directions: For each question, you will see a picture and you will hear four short statements. The statements will be spoken just one time. They will not be printed in your test book so you must listen carefully to understand what the speaker says. When you hear the four statements, look at the picture and choose the statement that best describes what you see in the picture. Choose the best answer (A), (B), (C), or (D).

EXAMPLE:

Now listen to the four statements. You will hear:

(A) He is on the phone.

(B) She is driving the car.

(C) She is typing on the computer.

(D) He is sitting next to her.

Statement (D) best describes what you see in the picture. Therefore, you should choose answer (D).

Sample Answer

A		B		C		D	✔

1

1. (A) ___ (B) ___ (C) ___ (D) ___

2. (A) ___ (B) ___ (C) ___ (D) ___

3. (A) ___ (B) ___ (C) ___ (D) ___

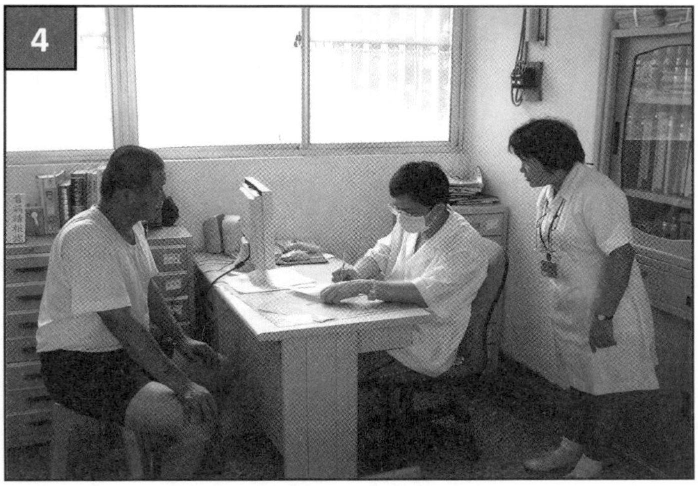

4. (A) ___ (B) ___ (C) ___ (D) ___

5

5. (A) ___ (B) ___ (C) ___ (D) ___

6

6. (A) ___ (B) ___ (C) ___ (D) ___

Part 2: Question–Response

Directions: In this part of the test, you will hear a question or statement spoken in English, followed by three responses, also spoken in English. The question or statement and the responses will be spoken just one time. They will not be printed in your test book, so you must listen carefully. You are to choose the best response to each question or statement. Now listen to a sample question.

You will hear: Man: Why are you late?
Woman: (A) I hope I won't be.
(B) My car broke down.
(C) He always is.

The best response is choice (B): "My car broke down". Therefore, you should choose (B).

7. (A) (B) (C)
8. (A) (B) (C)
9. (A) (B) (C)
10. (A) (B) (C)
11. (A) (B) (C)
12. (A) (B) (C)
13. (A) (B) (C)
14. (A) (B) (C)
15. (A) (B) (C)
16. (A) (B) (C)
17. (A) (B) (C)
18. (A) (B) (C)
19. (A) (B) (C)
20. (A) (B) (C)
21. (A) (B) (C)
22. (A) (B) (C)
23. (A) (B) (C)
24. (A) (B) (C)
25. (A) (B) (C)
26. (A) (B) (C)
27. (A) (B) (C)
28. (A) (B) (C)
29. (A) (B) (C)
30. (A) (B) (C)
31. (A) (B) (C)

Part 3: Conversations

Directions: You will hear some conversations between two or more people. You will be asked to answer three questions about what the speakers say in each conversation. Select the best response to each question and mark the letter (A), (B), (C), or (D) on your answer sheet. The conversations will not be printed in your test book and will be spoken only one time.

32. Why doesn't the man fly to the conference?
(A) It's only a seven-hour drive.
(B) It would take longer than driving.
(C) Because of bad weather.
(D) His company won't reimburse an airline ticket.

33. How would the man have gotten from the airport to the conference center?
(A) by bus
(B) by tram
(C) by plane
(D) by car

34. Why should the man keep track of his mileage?
(A) so he knows exactly how far he has driven
(B) so he can be more alert on the road
(C) so his company can pay him for his travel expenses
(D) so he can afford to drive back to his original destination

---

35. Where are they?
(A) a hotel
(B) a convenience store
(C) a restaurant
(D) a bakery

36. Why did the men want to speak to the manager?
(A) to complain about the service
(B) to praise the service
(C) to change their order
(D) to ask for a new server

37. What will the woman do after talking to the men?
(A) fire Gus
(B) let the men take their meal to their house
(C) give the men free dessert
(D) give the men the food they actually ordered

---

38. Who are the men in relationship to the woman?
(A) her possible employers
(B) her current bosses
(C) her references
(D) candidates for a position

39. Why did the man ask the woman why she should get the job?
(A) He wants to help her state her strengths.
(B) He wasn't certain if she was committed to it.
(C) The answer wasn't clear in her resume.
(D) Her references gave her a poor review.

40. How does the woman feel about working long hours?
(A) She thinks everyone should want to do it.
(B) She is eager to do it.
(C) She is not willing to do it.
(D) She is hesitant but willing to commit to it.

---

41. Where is the woman?
(A) in the office talking to George
(B) in her car talking on her cell phone
(C) in a meeting with Colleen
(D) in her bedroom at her house

42. What is going to happen with the curriculum change meeting?
(A) It has to be canceled indefinitely.
(B) It will be rescheduled for a later time.
(C) George will attend the meeting instead of Moira.
(D) Moira will go regardless of her illness because it is urgent.

43. What does the man promise to the woman?
(A) to call her on her cell phone in case of an emergency
(B) to prevent people from calling her
(C) to explain the new curriculum changes to everyone
(D) to take all of her phone messages

44. Who are the man and woman?
(A) parents
(B) husband and wife
(C) college students
(D) professors

45. What is the man worried about?
(A) Tony will never select a major in college.
(B) Tony will resent his interference.
(C) Tony won't earn enough money in the future.
(D) Tony doesn't love college as much as Tim.

46. What does the woman think?
(A) Her son needs to come home more often.
(B) The man should give Tony career advice.
(C) Her son should rethink his major.
(D) The man should let Tony make his own choices.

---

47. Why does the woman want a new computer?
(A) The one she has now is outdated.
(B) She just got a new job as a journalist.
(C) The one she owned previously no longer works.
(D) She enjoys staying up to date with technological advances.

48. Look at the graphic. Which computer is the woman likely to get?
(A) HC895 (C) MC1000
(B) CEL675 (D) DR234

49. Why does the man ask the woman a question?
(A) to understand what happened to her old computer
(B) to be able to recommend the most appropriate computer
(C) to learn who can best help meet her needs
(D) to get an idea of what kind of technological knowledge she possesses

MODEL	TYPE	SUITABLE FOR	PRICE
HC895	desktop	gaming	$150
CEL675	laptop	basic users	$200
MC1000	desktop	advanced multitasking	$400
DR234	laptop	presentations	$300

---

50. Why does the man stop by the woman's desk?
(A) He knows she is overwhelmed with work.
(B) He wants to confirm their lunch plans.
(C) He wants to explain the workings of the office to her.
(D) He wants to help her feel comfortable.

51. Why does the woman say, "It's a bit overwhelming."?
(A) She feels stressed trying to get used to her new tasks.
(B) It's the worst day of work she's ever had.
(C) She wishes people would be a little more welcoming.
(D) She wishes she had taken a different job offer.

52. What is the man's opinion of the cafeteria food?
(A) It's full of delicious treats.
(B) It's tastier than one might expect.
(C) He'd rather go somewhere else for lunch.
(D) It's not very appetizing.

---

53. Where are they?
(A) in a library (C) at a music store
(B) at a birthday party (D) at a bookstore

54. What will the woman probably do?
(A) buy a Jane Austen book
(B) buy *A Tale of Two Cities* from the Woodbury store
(C) wait five to seven days for the order to come in
(D) buy *Oliver Twist* instead

55. Why does the man suggest another store?
(A) It's a short trip.
(B) They are in charge of ordering books.
(C) It's the only way to get the desired book in time.
(D) They carry a larger variety of classic authors.

---

56. What is NOT a reason why the man wants to retire?
(A) He wants to travel.
(B) He's tired of working.
(C) He doesn't like his job anymore.
(D) He wants to do home repairs.

57. What is the woman's opinion on retiring?
(A) The man truly deserves it.
(B) They need to plan for it better.
(C) She's going to miss her job.
(D) It's too early to start talking about it.

58. What does the woman imply when she says, "You're always napping on the couch!"?
(A) The man has more time on his hands than he admits.
(B) The man is too lazy to accomplish his post-retirement goals.
(C) The man's job isn't very interesting.
(D) The man should work more if he wants to retire early.

59. What time did the woman arrive at the doctor's office?
(A) 3.30 (C) 2.30
(B) 3.10 (D) 4.30

60. Why did the woman arrive at the office at the time she did?
(A) She wanted to get in early so she would have time to run errands.
(B) She was already at a nearby coffee shop.
(C) She didn't want to leave the area and then return again.
(D) She likes to be punctual for appointments.

61. What is the woman going to do while waiting for her appointment?
(A) read a book
(B) watch television
(C) return home
(D) leaf through a magazine

---

62. What didn't the man have at the last conference?
(A) credit cards (C) a computer
(B) luggage (D) his passport

63. When will the man phone?
(A) as soon as he arrives
(B) later, when he is free
(C) the next morning
(D) just before his meeting

64. What is the relationship between the speakers?
(A) husband and wife
(B) friends
(C) colleagues
(D) boss and employee

---

65. Where is the man?
(A) in the woman's home
(B) on the phone
(C) with the woman in a shop
(D) in the woman's office

66. What was the problem?
(A) The computer wasn't connected to the electricity supply.
(B) The mouse was broken.
(C) The computer crashed.
(D) They couldn't find out what was wrong with it.

67. How does the man react?
(A) angrily
(B) in a funny way
(C) in an unfriendly way
(D) with patience

---

68. What is wrong with Ben?
(A) The bad weather stopped him from going to work.
(B) He is in a meeting.
(C) He is sick.
(D) He has to go away.

69. What will happen about the meeting?
(A) They'll hold it without Ben.
(B) It will be canceled completely.
(C) It will be postponed until a later date.
(D) Ben will rearrange it.

70. Why does the man say, "I owe you one."?
(A) He must give Susan her money back.
(B) He will help Susan in the future.
(C) Susan did the Jameson project for him.
(D) He stood Susan up on a date.

Part 4: Talks

Directions: You will hear some talks given by a single speaker. You will be asked to answer three questions about what the speaker says in each talk. Select the best response to each question and mark the letter (A), (B), (C), or (D) on your answer sheet. The talks will not be printed in your test book and will be spoken only one time.

Checklist for ideal business location: COFFEE HOUSE		
1	residential + commercial zone	✔
2	underground + bus stop	✔
3	teenagers + young adults	✔
4		✔

71. What do all the people listening to the speech have in common?

(A) They all want to start their own business.

(B) They are all employed by the speaker.

(C) They all own businesses in the community.

(D) They are all high-end retailers.

72. Look at the graphic. Which is likely to be the fourth point considered?

(A) low rent

(B) large space

(C) no coffee house within a mile

(D) lack of experienced staff

73. Why are people in high-income houses in the neighborhood important?

(A) They prevent interference of direct competitors.

(B) They have enough money to sustain the business.

(C) They do not have problems with transportation.

(D) They adhere to local zoning laws.

---

74. What happened in Oklahoma?

(A) The weather was surprisingly mild and calm.

(B) Many people were crippled by a dangerous storm.

(C) People were trapped in their homes due to a heavy snow storm.

(D) People were without electricity.

75. Where should you go if you want to see snow?

(A) north

(B) south

(C) east

(D) west

Twin Cities: Friday 29/6
37°C/99°F
Sunny
Precipitation: 0%
Wind: 10km/h
Excessive Heat Warning

76. Look at the graphic. What can be concluded about the weather in Twin Cities?

(A) It is highly variable.

(B) It is dry most of the time.

(C) There are no extreme temperatures.

(D) Precipitation is low throughout the year.

---

77. What does the speaker guarantee to the listeners?

(A) His speech will be interesting.

(B) He will not talk very long.

(C) He will delight them with the news he has.

(D) Working on the spacecraft center will take effort.

78. What has their work already accomplished?

(A) It has already made Houston the furthest outpost on the new frontier of science and space.

(B) It has made Houston the largest scientific and engineering community.

(C) Houston has joined forces with cities all over the world.

(D) It has generated new positions in the field.

79. What will happen to Houston?

(A) It will play a vital role in the space effort.

(B) It will be home to the newest scientific community.

(C) It will construct the Manned Spacecraft Center in the city center.

(D) It will create new frontiers to keep the economy afloat.

80. What is NOT true of the meal being prepared?
(A) It contains two types of olives.
(B) It's good for your health.
(C) It takes a lot of time to make.
(D) It's very tasty.

81. What needs to be put over heat?
(A) onions
(B) nuts
(C) the sauce
(D) the final product

82. What is being prepared?
(A) a seafood platter
(B) a seasoned steak
(C) a cherry tomato sauce
(D) a salad dish

---

83. What is the point of the speech?
(A) to explain how to write a research paper
(B) to criticize someone's speech
(C) to advise people on how to speak to a crowd
(D) to persuade the audience to become public speakers

84. What should speakers do with their notes?
(A) read them word by word
(B) memorize them so they don't have to hold them
(C) look at them for an extended amount of time beforehand
(D) look at them occasionally

85. What should speakers do if they make a mistake?
(A) correct it and continue
(B) ignore it and continue speaking
(C) apologize and then correct it
(D) excuse themselves and start the speech over again

---

86. Why does the speaker say, "Perhaps you need to work."?
(A) Some people cannot commit themselves fully to education.
(B) Work commitments may force some to drop out of college.
(C) Working people need to finish their education faster.
(D) College education can be very costly.

87. What type of class could you NOT take through the school?
(A) a class at 7:00 p.m. Wednesday
(B) an online class
(C) a Saturday morning business class
(D) a group session at your home

88. What part of the school does the advertisement focus on?
(A) the subjects that the school offers
(B) its ability to accommodate different lifestyles
(C) its past successes in educating a variety of people
(D) the quality of education the school offers

---

89. Why does the speaker say, "Thank you for your patience."?
(A) There is going to be an additional delay.
(B) The boarding process will take longer than usual.
(C) Some passengers will have to board another flight.
(D) There have been some mechanical issues with the plane.

90. What is NOT true of the plane?
(A) It is in Tampa, Florida.
(B) There will be no empty seats.
(C) It accommodates those with special needs.
(D) It has not yet taken off.

91. Why must passengers only board when called to do so?
(A) to abide by airline laws
(B) to avoid chaos
(C) because of the aircraft's mechanical problems
(D) to fill the flight to capacity

---

92. Where is this encounter taking place?
(A) at a food booth
(B) at Channel 8's studio
(C) near the fair's exit
(D) outside the man's car

93. What does Shelly work for?
(A) a radio station
(B) a newspaper
(C) a poll center
(D) a TV station

94. What highlight is Shelly especially interested in?
(A) his favorite ride
(B) his favorite food
(C) his favorite music concert
(D) his favorite TV channel

95. Where is this announcement taking place?
(A) Stowe Hall
(B) the Radcliffe Building
(C) the Olmstead Room
(D) the parking lot

96. When do the meetings normally conclude?
(A) 9.00
(B) 6.30
(C) 5.30
(D) 8.00

97. Look at the graphic. Which of the following would best describe the event?
(A) International Performers Convention
(B) Local Tech Experts Workshop
(C) Corporate Managers Meeting
(D) Overseas Teacher Training Workshop

Session 1	Effective Time Management
Session 2	Enhancing Student Performance
Session 3	Digital Tools in Learning
Session 4	Managing Behavior Problems

98. What is NOT something the audience should refrain from?
(A) taking pictures with a flash
(B) leaving for the bathroom during the performance
(C) answering their cellular phones
(D) leaving when there is an emergency

99. What does the speaker give directions for?
(A) the refreshment stand
(B) the restrooms
(C) the lobby
(D) the auditorium entrance

100. What will the actors be doing after the performance?
(A) changing out of costume
(B) snacking and socializing
(C) signing and posing
(D) answering questions

Vocabulary Development for Test 3, Reading, Parts 5 & 6

illegible (adj): difficult or impossible to read

illimitable (adj): without limits

bypass (v): to go around something in order to avoid it

appoint (v): to choose someone for a job

gratuity (n): a tip, money given to someone for providing a service

amid (prep): in the middle of something

twin (v): to join two things together; to link

comrade (n): a friend that you work with, or were soldiers together with during a war

solely (adv): only, exclusively

expedition (n): an organized trip for a particular purpose

audacity (n): shocking and rude behavior

outwit (v): to act cleverer than another person and get an advantage from that

surrogate (adj): replacing someone else

cockeyed (adj): ridiculous; completely unreasonable

ingenious (adj): very clever and resourceful

grifter (n): a person who gets money by tricking people

omit (v): to not include something, neglect

proliferation (n): an increase in something

absentee (n): someone who is not where they are supposed to be

eminent (adj): well known

immense (adj): huge

resentment (n): the feeling of anger because someone has forced you to accept something you don't like

Vocabulary Development for Test 3, Reading, Parts 5 & 6

Exercise A

Choose the correct answer, (A), (B), or (C), to complete the sentences.

1. The problems of inflation and unemployment still cause a lot of ....

   (A) resentment (C) expedition

   (B) gratuity

2. We had to take the road that .... the town to avoid the traffic.

   (A) appoints (C) outwits

   (B) bypasses

3. She is a(n) .... and highly respected doctor.

   (A) cockeyed (C) illimitable

   (B) eminent

4. There are several .... from college this week, because a lot of people have the flu.

   (A) comrades (C) absentees

   (B) grifters

Exercise B

Choose the correct word, (A), (B), or (C), to fill the gaps in the text.

I am so annoyed with Samantha! She wrote the note, not me. And it's not my fault that her writing is almost **(5)** .... and the director arrived at the meeting at the wrong time. But she had the **(6)** .... to blame me for her mistake! And nobody will believe me because everybody wants to be nice to her. You see, she's just been **(7)** .... as an assistant director of the Publishing Division.

5. (A) illegible (B) ingenious (C) illimitable
6. (A) grifter (B) audacity (C) proliferation
7. (A) outwitted (B) twinned (C) appointed

Exercise C

Complete the sentences using the correct form of three of the words in the box below.

surrogate	immense	solely	amid	gratuity
ingenious	eminent	illimitable	cockeyed	illegible

8. The mechanic spent a(n) .... amount of time getting the engine into perfect condition.
9. Because they had no children of their own, their nephew became a kind of .... child to them.
10. Do you really expect us to believe a(n) .... story like that?

SECTION 2

Reading

In the Reading test, you will read a variety of texts and answer several different types of reading comprehension questions. The entire Reading test will last 75 minutes. There are three parts, and directions are given for each part. You are encouraged to answer as many questions as possible within the time allowed. You must mark your answers on the separate answer sheet. Do not write your answers in your test book.

Part 5: Incomplete Sentences

Directions: A word or phrase is missing in each of the sentences below. Four answer choices are given below each sentence. Select the best answer to complete the sentence. Then mark the letter (A), (B), (C), or (D) on your answer sheet.

Example: Her boss was talking to her ....
(A) angry (B) friendly (C) angrily (D) unfriendly Correct answer: (C)

101. Jerry was surprised that the projects were completed .... quickly.
(A) almost (C) much
(B) so (D) too

102. The company must .... 50 new employees by September 15th next year.
(A) be hired (C) hire
(B) have hired (D) to hire

103. Unfortunately, due to the company's financial problems, they will have to severely .... on staff.
(A) cut back (C) fall down
(B) look out (D) fire off

104. Personal phone calls .... from the office telephone.
(A) will not consent
(B) have no permission
(C) cannot be made
(D) haven't allowed

105. Jack said that he couldn't read his colleague's note because his handwriting was ....
(A) illiterate (C) illuminated
(B) illegible (D) illimitable

106. We cleaned the restaurant all night in order to .... all the health code regulations.
(A) defeat (C) originate
(B) satisfy (D) bypass

107. Rarely .... in the stock market.
(A) he invests (C) does he invest
(B) he does invest (D) he has invested

108. .... our competitors, our store is open 24 hours a day for your convenience.
(A) Unlike (C) Likely to
(B) Instead of (D) Similar

109. If your subscription to *USA Today* expires, you may .... it online.
(A) renew (C) repossess
(B) reveal (D) renovate

110. Kate Fox has been .... to the board of directors.
(A) designed (C) campaigned
(B) appointed (D) contacted

111. All the sponsors .... by the organization president.
(A) will be acknowledged
(B) will acknowledge
(C) acknowledged
(D) acknowledging

112. .... consumer demand, our products will be packaged using recycled products.
(A) Therefore
(B) Due to the fact that
(C) Because
(D) In response to

113. This state-of-the-art computer comes with a two-year .... of quality.

(A) grant (C) gratuity
(B) guardian (D) guarantee

114. So far, everyone who's heard the news about Gerry's appointment as head of sales is thrilled ....

(A) about them (C) about it
(B) by them (D) by then

115. Establishing a good working relationship .... management and the workforce is a challenge.

(A) between (C) amid
(B) beside (D) inside

116. Productivity has fallen dramatically during the last three years and is struggling to ....

(A) catch back (C) catch for
(B) catch up (D) catch in

117. The conference's turnout has nearly .... in the last few years.

(A) twinned (C) replicated
(B) twice (D) doubled

118. The regional vice president is .... conducting company evaluations.

(A) delegated for (C) in charge of
(B) responsible to (D) obligated by

119. Although my office is nicely decorated, it is too small for my filing cabinet .... desk chair.

(A) nor (C) thus
(B) and (D) but

120. This new tablet was very expensive, so please handle it with ....

(A) care (C) carefully
(B) careful (D) carelessness

121. Ms Barton's .... will explain the details of the new mail policy.

(A) accomplice (C) commuter
(B) assistant (D) client

122. .... possible, Mr Brown tries to visit all of the company's offices.

(A) Whether (C) Whenever
(B) Whatever (D) Whichever

123 .... Mr Arnold replace Mr Dendler, his salary would be doubled.

(A) Were (C) However
(B) Although (D) Should

124. Mr Cook is .... responsible for any debts the company may incur.

(A) solely (C) unique
(B) lonely (D) individual

125. The conference room .... for the meeting was on the sixth floor.

(A) selected him (C) he selected
(B) which selected (D) that selected

126. The two electrical companies announced plans for a joint ....

(A) venture (C) conversion
(B) apparition (D) advantage

127. Henry .... last week from conductor to supervisor.

(A) promoted (C) was promoted
(B) had promoted (D) was promoting

128. The manager ordered new uniforms for the .... last month.

(A) personal (C) stuff
(B) staff (D) shareholders

129. Every once .... a while, Patrick treats his customers to a free dessert.

(A) in (C) to
(B) for (D) until

130. Please list your email address and WhatsApp number with all ....

(A) persuasion (C) expedition
(B) correspondence (D) commotion

Part 6: Text Completion

Directions: Read the texts that follow. A word or phrase is missing in some of the sentences. Four answer choices are given below each of the sentences. Select the best answer to complete the text. Then mark the letter (A), (B), (C), or (D) on your answer sheet.

Questions 131–134 refer to the following news story.

Once again, truth is stranger than fiction, and this enthralling cat-and-mouse game was .... by the exploits of audacious Frank W Abagnale Jr, known as the *Skywayman*. From the time he ran away from his troubled home at age 16, to his capture at 21, Abagnale passed himself off as a co-pilot on Pan Am, an emergency room physician, a lawyer, and a millionaire.

131. (A) inspired (B) retired (C) expired (D) wired

He was so skilled at 'paperhanging' (check fraud) – and had such audacity – that for years, he was able to outwit and outmaneuver FBI Agent Carl Hanratty, who patiently pursued him .... the world while developing a curious surrogate-father/son relationship with the daring identity thief.

132. (A) through (B) along (C) around (D) into

Perceptively directed by Steven Spielberg from Jeff Nathanson's expertly plotted screenplay, based on Abagnale's memoir, it's a cockeyed version of the American dream: an ingenious, jet-setting grifter who scammed bad checks in 50 states and 26 countries, bilking banks of $2.5 million, ... he's still haunted by the sins of his parents which fractured his family.

133. (A) despite (B) because (C) yet (D) whatsoever

After serving five years, Abagnale was released from prison on the condition that he teach law enforcement how to prevent fraud. ....

134. (A) He has thus returned to crime and seems unwilling to conform.
(B) This is why he is reluctant to assist in any investigation.
(C) Currently he spends most of his time in prison.
(D) Now he has his own security firm and lectures at the FBI Academy.

Questions 135–138 refer to the following article.

Most people plan financially long-term, but they don't have a long-term physical plan. They plan for retirement, but they don't prepare for what I call physical "re-firement" in the .... years in life. Re-firement is to ignite, to excite. That's where my energy comes from.

135. (A) finish (B) lately (C) later (D) end

The commitment

I wrestled on and off in high school. What I noticed was, when you're a wrestler, you're in the best condition of your life. But after the season, I'd go back to my lifestyle of overeating. Then we'd go back for practice and it was like hell week. You'd feel like you wanted to throw up. In 11th grade, I decided to never let myself get out of .... again. It's too much work.

136. (A) health (B) shape (C) fitness (D) grade

In the details

People aren't used to focusing .... their muscles the way I make them focus.

137. (A) on (B) in (C) with (D) over

It's attention to detail, never sacrificing your form for an extra repetition. If you do everything correctly, you'll have better results in a shorter .... of time.

138. (A) era (B) period (C) episode (D) part

Questions 139–142 refer to the following presentation.

I'm glad you are all here today. ...., the better communication we can have about issues that worry you, the easier it is for us to respond to problems. Governors are problem-solvers. And so is the President. .... And the best way to do so is in the spirit of cooperation.

139. (A) Precisely (C) Obviously
(B) Positively (D) Entirely

140. (A) Sometimes, though, problem-solving isn't easy.
(B) Our job is to identify problems and deal with them.
(C) However, communication is often limited between us.
(D) And if all of us act independently, we thrive.

That's sometimes hard in Washington, I readily admit. This is not a town that thrives upon cooperation, like most state capitals. But we'll .... to work hard to help you, because by helping our governors, we really help our people. And that's the job of a president.

141. (A) follow (C) maintain
(B) continue (D) remain

Yesterday, in my toast, I said the war on drugs goes on, and it does. I wish I .... otherwise, but that's not a true assessment of the world. We are chasing the Mafia; we're dealing with criminals and proliferation. But this war still goes on. It's very important for you to know that.

142. (A) could report (C) should report
(B) am reporting (D) might report

Questions 143–146 refer to the following article.

Absentee landlords were a highly .... issue in the history of Ireland. During the course of the 16th and 17th centuries, most of the land in Ireland was confiscated from Irish Catholic landowners during the Plantation of Ireland and granted to British settlers.

143. (A) significant (C) eminent
(B) considerable (D) immense

Seized land was given to English nobles and soldiers, some of .... rented it out to Irishmen while they remained residents of England. Over the centuries, resentment grew as not only were the absentee landlords Protestant (while most tenants were Catholic), but their existence meant that the wealth of the land was always exported.

144. (A) whose (C) that
(B) who (D) whom

In the years .... the Irish Potato Famine, the land issue with the Irish Land League's Land War had become extremely important in Ireland.

145. (A) that following (C) following
(B) followed (D) had followed

The land issue was one of the historic factors that .... Ireland's troubled history to this day.

146. (A) resulted in (C) caused to
(B) demanded of (D) enlarged on

Vocabulary Development for Test 3, Reading, Part 7

domestic (adj): relating to a person's own country

leap (v): to increase, improve, or grow very quickly

incompatible: (adj) not able to exist or work with another person or thing because of basic differences

freelance (adj): doing different projects for different companies instead of working all the time for a single company

cultivate (v): if you cultivate a relationship, you make a special effort to establish and develop it because you think it might be useful to you

obtain (v): to get something, especially by asking for it, buying it, or producing it from something else

drawback (n): a disadvantage, or the negative part of a situation

outweigh (v): to be greater or more important than something else

rigorous (adj): strict or severe

attire (n): clothes, especially of a particular or formal type

versatile (adj): able to change easily from one activity to another, able to be used for many different purposes

accomplishment: (n) something that is achieved after a lot of work or effort

luxurious (adj): very comfortable and expensive

contain (v): to keep something harmful within limits and not allow it to spread

inflation (n): a general increase in prices and fall in the purchasing value of money

unveil (v): if you unveil something new, you show it or make it known for the first time

compelling (adj): if a reason, argument, etc., is compelling, it makes you believe it or accept it because it is so strong

comprehensive: (adj) complete and including everything that is necessary; wide-ranging

curriculum (n): the subjects studied in a school, college, etc., and what each subject includes

eligible (adj): having the necessary qualities or satisfying the necessary conditions

Vocabulary Development for Test 3, Reading, Part 7

Exercise A

Choose the correct answer, (A), (B), or (C), to complete the sentences.

1. I think you are .... for early retirement. You really need to look into it.

(A) eligible
(B) comprehensive
(C) compelling

2. There is a significant reduction in annual .... from 24% to 17%.

(A) attire
(B) accomplishment
(C) inflation

3. The company has recently .... plans to modernize the production process.

(A) leaped
(B) unveiled
(C) contained

4. We want all our staff to be .... as it's often required to cover for somebody else.

(A) incompatible
(B) domestic
(C) versatile

Exercise B

Choose the correct word, (A), (B), or (C), to fill the gaps in the text.

Jack is the kind of person who is never happy. When he did office work, he said that it was too boring and he hated working 9 to 5. So, he decided to work as a(n) **(5)** .... photographer. He did a course on photography first, and then started working as a photographer.

Now he isn't particularly happy about his new role and he says that the disadvantages **(6)** .... the advantages, and the main **(7)** .... is that he has to drive to different places all the time.

5. (A) freelance (B) incompatible (C) luxurious

6. (A) leap (B) cultivate (C) outweigh

7. (A) attire (B) drawback (C) curriculum

Exercise C

Complete the sentences using the correct form of three of the words in the box below.

leap	luxurious	outweigh	rigorous	comprehensive
obtain	domestic	incompatible	eligible	compelling

8. Shares in the company .... by 80 per cent.

9. We do know that maintaining quality is .... with increasing output.

10. A(n) .... monetary and fiscal policy is more likely to encourage efficiency.

Part 7: Reading Comprehension

Directions: You will read a selection of texts, such as magazine and newspaper articles, letters, and advertisements. Each text is followed by several questions. Select the best answer for each question and mark the letter (A), (B), (C), or (D) on your answer sheet.

Example: Are you someone who enjoys trying new things and does not feel uncomfortable in new environments? Then why not get paid for it? *CULTURE* magazine is looking for individuals to go to new clubs, events, etc., and write about the cultural scene they observe in these places. Interested? Send your resume to CULTURE@hotmail.com. Please, no phone calls.

What type of person would be best qualified for this job?

(A) a homebird (B) an introvert (C) a clumsy person (D) a risk-taker Correct answer: (D)

Questions 147–149 refer to the following advertisement.

ALL TRAILS LEAD TO THE SUNSET GRILLE AND TAP ROOM

Lakeville's favorite family restaurant!

WESTERN-STYLE BARBECUE

***STEAKS *RIBS *SEAFOOD *GREAT KIDS' MENU**

✦ 10 dinners under $10!
✦ Satellite sports on multiple TVs and our big screen
✦ Ski videos, games, old-style CD jukebox
✦ Lakeville's largest domestic beer selection

Open 7 days a week: lunch, dinner, late-night, and take-out

** For this week only, come with a party of eight or more and we will throw in a free dessert for everyone! Why not treat your company staff to a morale-boosting lunch?

"... To find a spot that both the locals and your pocket can feel comfortable with ... you'll need the Sunset Grille."
Brackets Crossing Magazine, September issue

147. What is the limited offer?

(A) A party will be thrown every day for a week.

(B) Satellite sports will be shown on the big screen.

(C) free desserts for those who come with a lot of people

(D) the amount of domestic beers being sold

148. Who are probably the most suitable customers for this restaurant?

(A) retired people

(B) parents and their children

(C) people with a lot of money

(D) party planners

149. What time would the restaurant probably NOT be open?

(A) 10.00 p.m.

(B) 4.30 p.m.

(C) noon

(D) 9.30 a.m.

Questions 150–153 refer to the following newspaper article.

NEW YORK Stock Exchange

NEW YORK Stock Exchange – A barrel of light, sweet crude for February delivery dropped $1.75, to $50.49, in midday trading on the New York Mercantile Exchange. Prices dropped as low as $50.05, their lowest since May 25th, shortly after the inventory report's release by the federal Energy Information Administration.

U.S. crude oil stocks leaped by 6.8 million barrels, to 321.5 million, when analysts had been expecting an increase of just 325,000 barrels, according to a Dow Jones Newswires Survey. The EIA also said that inventories are above the upper end of the average range for this time of year.

Motor gasoline inventories, meanwhile, rose by 3.5 million barrels, to 216.8 million, above analysts' expectations of a 2.6 million barrel rise. Distillate stocks, including heating oil and diesel fuel, rose by 900,000 barrels, to 141.9 million barrels, compared with analysts' expectations of a 1.3 million barrel rise.

150. What was the original price of the sweet crude mentioned in the first paragraph?

(A) $50.49

(B) $52.24

(C) $48.74

(D) $51.80

151. How big of an increase in crude oil stocks was predicted?

(A) 325,000 barrels

(B) 6.8 million barrels

(C) 1.3 million barrels

(D) 321.5 million barrels

152. What is the source that has provided the actual inventory results?

(A) the Dow Jones Newswires Survey

(B) the New York Mercantile Exchange

(C) the state Government

(D) the Energy Information Administration

153. What is true of the inventory numbers?

(A) All the prices dropped.

(B) They are all higher than expected.

(C) They are incompatible with predictions.

(D) They are the lowest they've been since May 25th.

Questions 154–157 refer to the following leaflet.

FREELANCE BENEFITS AND DRAWBACKS

Freelancers generally enjoy a greater variety of assignments than in regular employment, and almost always have more freedom to choose their work schedule. The experience also allows the opportunity to build up a portfolio of work and cultivate a network of clients in hopes of obtaining a permanent position.

A major drawback is the uncertainty of work – and thus income – and lack of company benefits, such as health insurance or retirement pay.

Another drawback is that freelancers often must handle contracts, legal issues, accounting, marketing, and other business functions by themselves. If they do choose to pay for professional services, they can sometimes turn into significant out-of-pocket expenses, usually passed on to the client, which is generally not welcome. Finally, working hours can extend beyond the standard working day and working week.

154. What does freelancing afford?

(A) regular employment

(B) an assortment of projects

(C) freedom to refuse a permanent position

(D) opportunities to employ clients

155. What could possibly be a negative aspect of freelance work?

(A) an unimpressive portfolio

(B) not receiving retirement pay

(C) a possibility of not earning enough money

(D) having less freedom

156. If freelancers decide they need somebody to help them,

(A) they won't be able to make any money.

(B) they will have the same advantages as if they own a company.

(C) the quality of their work will be affected.

(D) their clients won't be pleased.

157. What is the purpose of this leaflet?

(A) to balance the pros and cons of freelance work

(B) to encourage professionals to freelance

(C) to show how the negatives outweigh the positives in freelancing

(D) to give a detailed definition of freelance work

Questions 158–160 refer to the following brochure.

WHAT YOUR CLOTHES SAY ABOUT YOU AT A JOB INTERVIEW

- Appropriate attire supports your image as a person who takes the interview process seriously and understands the nature of the industry in which you are trying to become employed.
- Be aware that, in some industries, customer contact and image presented to the customer are vital. **-[1]-** In such industries, your attire will be judged more critically.
- Your attire should be noticed as being appropriate and well-fitting, but it should not take center stage.
- If you are primarily remembered for your interview attire, this is probably because you made an error in judgment! **-[2]-**
- Dressing nicely and appropriately is a compliment to the person you meet, so if in doubt, err on the side of dressing better than you might need to.
- Even if you are aware that employees of an organization dress casually on the job, dress up for the interview unless you are specifically told otherwise by the employer.
- Never confuse an interview or business function with a social event. **-[3]-**.
- Not every contact with an employer requires interview attire. **-[4]-** For some occasions, business casual is appropriate. See business casual for what it is and when to wear it.

158. What does it mean if the interviewer remembers your outfit better than anything?

(A) You must have dressed inappropriately.

(B) You complimented the interviewer.

(C) You dressed appropriately.

(D) You were judged unfairly.

159. What should you do if you know the employees where you are being interviewed dress casually?

(A) Call ahead of time and ask the employer what to wear.

(B) Find a way to dress similarly to the employees.

(C) Wear clothes that say you are a person who takes this process seriously.

(D) Dress in a way that shows you are not aware of what employees wear.

160. In which of the positions marked [1], [2], [3], and [4] does the following sentence best belong? "Don't dress for a party or a date."

(A) [1]

(B) [2]

(C) [3]

(D) [4]

Questions 161–163 refer to the following sports magazine article.

PLAYER BIO: MEGHAN MONTGOMERY

She was an All-Big Ten first team selection, an Academic All-Big Ten, and was voted team captain for a second straight season. She's a versatile athlete who played and started at outside back, outside midfield, and forward. Meghan left Purdue as its all-time leader, with 84 matches played, and she is one of only four Boilermakers to play in over 80 matches. She broke the program record for matches played with a start against Ohio State in the first round of the Big Ten Tournament and was one of only two Boilermakers to play and start in all 20 matches.

She set personal season bests in several offensive categories, including shots, shots on goal, goals, and points scored. She was the first and only Big Ten player to score against Penn State during the regular season and scored against the Nittany Lions in the eighth minute off a midfield assist from Parrissa Eyorokon.

161. Why is Montgomery described as a versatile athlete?
- (A) She can do many things.
- (B) She is determined.
- (C) She is a good leader.
- (D) She has broken records.

162. How many Boilermakers have played in at least 80 matches?
- (A) one
- (B) three
- (C) four
- (D) five

163. When did Montgomery break the record for matches played?
- (A) her first game against Ohio State
- (B) the second season
- (C) the championship of a tournament
- (D) one of the first games of a tournament

Questions 164–167 refer to the following leaflet.

INTERVIEW TIP 1: PLAN AHEAD – Do a little homework! Research the company and the position if possible. Review your work experience and be ready to support past career accomplishments with specific information targeted toward the company's needs.

INTERVIEW TIP 2: ROLE-PLAY – Once you have finished studying, begin role-playing (rehearsing). Use the general questions provided below in the Interview Preparation Area. Write down answers if it helps to make your presentation more concise. Try to limit your answers to the information your new employer will want to know.

INTERVIEW TIP 3: ADAPT – Be sensitive to the style of the interviewer. Pay attention to those details of dress, office furniture, and general decor, which will afford helpful clues to assist you in tailoring your presentation.

INTERVIEW TIP 4: RELATE – Try to relate your answers to the interviewer and his or her company. Focus on achievements relevant to the position.

INTERVIEW TIP 5: ENCOURAGE – Encourage the interviewer to share information about his or her company. Demonstrate your interest.

164. What is the point of Tip 1?
- (A) to ensure you remember the position offered
- (B) to find a way to link your experience to what the company wants
- (C) to improve your research skills before the interview
- (D) to tailor your resume with appropriate past experiences

165. In which tip is it suggested that you should pretend that you are being interviewed?
- (A) Tip 4
- (B) Tip 3
- (C) Tip 1
- (D) Tip 2

166. In which tip is it suggested that you provoke answers from the interviewer?
- (A) Tip 3
- (B) Tip 5
- (C) Tip 1
- (D) Tip 2

167. Why should you pay attention to office furniture?
- (A) It could suggest how to modify your questions.
- (B) It could tell you if you are an appropriate candidate.
- (C) It could suggest how much money you would earn.
- (D) It could tell you if you need to adapt your presentation.

Questions 168–169 refer to the following card.

The Hotel
801 Collins Avenue
Miami Beach, Florida 33139
Tel: 305 531 2222 – Fax: 305 531 3222

In the heart of South Beach is an art deco hotel where high style meets history, luxurious accommodation is filled with warmth, and AAA Four Diamond award-winning hospitality and service are second to none.

Fully equipped conference rooms are also available.

168. Where would this card most likely be found?
(A) in a tourist office
(B) in a hotel room
(C) in an office building
(D) in a restaurant

169. What is the purpose of this card?
(A) to ask for information
(B) to attract customers
(C) to announce an event
(D) to make an introduction

Questions 170–171 refer to the following news report.

NEWS

Australia has seen its jobless rate fall to its lowest level in 33 years in September, official data shows, raising chances of an interest rate rise.

Employers created 13,000 new jobs for the month, sending the unemployment rate down to 4.2%, from 4.3%. The job rise was lower than forecast but came after August's figures were revised significantly up, by 34,300.

The government raised interest rates to their highest in 10 years in August, to 6.5%, in a bid to contain inflation.

170. What is true about jobs in Australia?
(A) There are fewer now than there have been in more than 30 years.
(B) There are more now than there have been in more than 30 years.
(C) There were more than were expected.
(D) They are not related to interest rates at all.

171. In what section of an Australian newspaper would this article most likely be found?
(A) the international section
(B) the sports section
(C) the cultural section
(D) the financial section

Questions 172–173 refer to the following notice.

Do You Need Office Space?

If you are looking to lease, rent, or buy office space, you've come to the right place! Since our start in 2015, the OfficeFinder™ team has personally assisted requests from over 140,000 businesses of all sizes looking for office space. If your goal is to find the right office space, make sure you get the best deal possible. To avoid costly mistakes, we can help with our network of local professionals in over 450 markets!

172. Who would be most interested in this notice?
(A) someone who wants a job
(B) someone starting a business
(C) someone who works remotely
(D) someone involved in marketing

173. What is implied about choosing the wrong office?
(A) It could ruin your career.
(B) It could be expensive.
(C) It is very easy to do.
(D) It can disrupt the network.

Questions 174–175 refer to the following text message chain.

Karen Mathews 9.24
Hi, Paul. There's been a change of plans, I'm afraid. I'll be arriving much later in the evening. You need to call Mr Brown.

Paul Leeds 9.27
OK, then, I'll ask him to reschedule for tomorrow, just to be sure. I know how important this deal is for you. I hope there is nothing serious going on, though.

Karen Mathews 9.30
Weather here is terrible and all flights have been delayed. I've been stuck in the airport for the past four hours. No idea when we'll be able to fly out.

Paul Leeds 9.32
Oh, that's terrible. So, let us know as soon as there is an update so we can arrange someone to pick you up from the airport.

Karen Mathews 9.34
Not necessary. Mr Dean has arranged for a taxi to get me directly to HQ, no matter what time I arrive.

Paul Leeds 9.37
I wasn't aware of that. All right, we'll be in touch. Fly safe!

174. Why is the woman texting the man?
(A) Her flight was canceled.
(B) She will arrive a day later than expected.
(C) She needs the man to put off a meeting.
(D) She wants someone to get her from the airport.

175. At 9.34, why does Karen write, "Not necessary."?
(A) They don't need to send someone to the airport.
(B) She doesn't have to update the man.
(C) She doesn't have to go straight to the office.
(D) There is no need to complain about the weather.

Questions 176–180 refer to the following classified and cover letter.

ANNOUNCEMENT OF VACANCY

Track & Field Head Coach

Millbrook High School

The **Frederick County** School System is seeking applications for the position of Track & Field Head Coach at **Millbrook High School**. This award-winning, highly successful school division cares deeply for its students and staff, maintains modern facilities, has a comprehensive curriculum, and offers a wide range of programs, including regional special education and a number of vocational/education offerings.

Millbrook High School is a 9th- through 12th-grade facility, with a student population of approximately 1,500.

Qualifications:

- Successful coaching experience in the sport required.
- Eligible for or holding a Virginia License, with a secondary education endorsement preferred.

Responsibilities:

The position requires developing and maintaining an in-school recruiting program, developing a positive rapport with the school staff and community, working cooperatively with the coordinator of student activities and school administration, and establishing and coordinating the coaching duties and responsibilities of the coaching staff.

Chris Saffert
757 Raymond Ave.
Millbrook, VA 55114
April 7th

To Whom It May Concern:

I am writing to apply for the Track & Field Head Coach position at Millbrook High School. Attached, you will find my resume, which lists all of my past work experience and qualifications in greater detail.

As you can see, I was Head Coach at Lakeville Senior High School for seven years before I moved to Virginia. When I first started there, the team had never won an event, let alone an entire meet, but during my time there they eventually won the state championship. Apart from necessary recruiting, I firmly believe that, with the appropriate training and encouragement, all student athletes can be successful.

Lastly, as I have only just moved to Virginia, I do not possess a Virginia License, but I do possess the Iowa equivalent. I am therefore qualified to be licensed here and I am in the process of obtaining a license. I will not have a secondary education endorsement on the license. Please call me if you have any questions.

Sincerely,
Chris Saffert

176. What is the purpose of the first paragraph in the *Announcement of Vacancy*?

(A) to illustrate the school's athletic achievements

(B) to reveal what the school's program is lacking

(C) to make the school seem appealing to applicants

(D) to state the school's hopes for the future

177. What is NOT a responsibility of the coaching position?

(A) hiring coaching staff

(B) working together with another professional

(C) having a good relationship with people

(D) getting students to join the team

178. Why doesn't Chris Saffert talk about all of his experience in this letter?

(A) That information is listed elsewhere.

(B) He didn't think it was necessary.

(C) He prefers to explain it over the phone.

(D) He probably forgot.

179. What may possibly hurt Chris Saffert during the selection process?

(A) his coaching record

(B) his license type

(C) his coaching philosophy

(D) his lack of professionalism

180. What was Chris Saffert's impact on the Lakeville Track & Field Team?

(A) He maintained their history of success.

(B) His beliefs upset the athletes.

(C) He increased their level of success.

(D) He couldn't get them to win a championship.

Questions 181–185 refer to the following instant message chain and attachment.

Kelly 11.10
Hi, Josh, I thought I'd forward you something to laugh about at your office.

Josh 11.12
That's so typical of you, Kelly! You know how much work I still have to do.

Kelly 11.14
But I don't think a short break should keep you from meeting your deadline!

Josh 11.16
Look, I have so much on my plate right now that even texting you back means I'm falling further behind. Plus, you know my workload isn't the same as yours.

Kelly 11.17
So I guess I shouldn't be coming downstairs for lunch break then, should I?

The sweet old couple

(Dangers of making assumptions: understand before you intervene)

A little old couple walked into a fast food restaurant. The little old man walked up to the counter, ordered the food, paid, and took the tray back to the table where the little old lady sat. On the tray there was a hamburger, a small bag of fries, and a drink. Carefully, the old man cut the hamburger in two and divided the fries into two neat piles. He sipped the drink and passed it to the little old lady, who took a sip and passed it back.

A young man on a nearby table had watched the old couple and felt sorry for them. He offered to buy them another meal, but the old man politely declined, saying that they were used to sharing everything. The old man began to eat his food, but his wife sat still, not eating. The young man continued to watch the couple. He still felt he should be offering to help. As the little old man finished eating, the old lady had still not started on her food. "Ma'am, why aren't you eating?" asked the young man sympathetically.

The old lady looked up and said politely, "Well, I'm waiting for the teeth."

181 Why is Josh working longer than normal?
(A) He needs to earn extra money.
(B) He wants to impress his boss.
(C) He wants to get ahead on his work before he goes on vacation.
(D) He has to turn something in at a scheduled date.

182. At 11.12, why does the man write "That's so typical of you, Kelly?"
(A) Kelly occasionally falls behind with her work.
(B) Kelly and the man have frequently argued over work.
(C) Kelly often distracts him at work.
(D) The man does not approve of Kelly's work.

183. How did Kelly deliver the note and story to Josh?
(A) She sent it to him by fax.
(B) She emailed it to him.
(C) She left it on his desk.
(D) She had it delivered by a courier.

184. How did the young man in the story feel when he first saw the couple?
(A) He felt pity for them and their situation.
(B) He was envious of their sweet relationship.
(C) He was perturbed by their public solicitation of food.
(D) He felt self-conscious that they were watching him eat.

185. What, besides their meal, is the couple in the story sharing?
(A) a toupee
(B) dentures
(C) a pair of eyeglasses
(D) a hearing aid

Questions 186–190 refer to the following letter, LinkedIn message, and classified.

To Whom It May Concern:

My name is Robert Thomas and I am interested in volunteering for your program. **-[1]-** However, I have a few questions I would like to ask before I make my final decision.

First of all, I am proficient in Spanish and would like to work in a Spanish-speaking country. **-[2]-** What Spanish-speaking countries does your program work in? I'm afraid those are the only ones I would be interested in.

Secondly, how long of a commitment would this be? Is it for a few weeks, the whole summer, for a year, or as long as you choose? **-[3]-** My preference is to work for the entire year, but I am flexible and I could adapt to your needs.

Finally, are there specific qualifications you are looking for? **-[4]-** However, I spent most of my academic career volunteering in the surrounding community. For example, I volunteered at a senior citizen living center.

You may respond to this letter by email or telephone. All my information is on the following page, along with a list of references.

Thank you for your time.

Sincerely,
Robert Thomas

Message on LinkedIn

To: Andrea Greening **[Sunnyview Carehome]**

Hi Andrea, I hope you don't mind. I've put you as a referee for a job that I'm applying for. If you could mention my companionship and recreational work, and maybe my first-aid skills, that would be great. Best avoid my kitchen duties!
Thanks, Rob.

Volunteer for International Service-Learning

Your service of 15–25 hours a week at an established agency, supervised by professionals, will make a difference to people in need.

Care for: the poor, the young, the disabled, the ill, the old, and the troubled

Teach: children, teens, adults; job skills, literacy, recreation, and ESL

Community development:
economic assistance, human rights, healthcare, cultural heritage, environment, and women's issues

186. What is Robert's opinion of where he prefers to work?

(A) He wants to go to Spain.
(B) He's afraid to go to another country.
(C) He has a preference, but would be happy anywhere.
(D) He is limited in where he is willing to go.

187. In which of the positions marked [1], [2], [3], and [4] does the following sentence best belong? "I am straight out of college and have no professional experience."

(A) [1]
(B) [2]
(C) [3]
(D) [4]

188. What would Rob prefer Andrea not to mention?

(A) his cooking
(B) his social skills
(C) his leisure activities
(D) his first-aid skills

189. Which of the program components does Robert have experience in?

(A) teaching teens
(B) working with environmentally safe living conditions
(C) caring for old people
(D) teaching recreation

190. What does the community development component entail?

(A) one-on-one mentoring with the poor
(B) dealing with broad social issues
(C) building homes in the community
(D) recruiting more people to volunteer

Questions 191–195 refer to the following email, attachment, and memo.

To: *SOCY101 Class*

Dear SOCY101 Class,

I thought that while you were writing your final papers, it might interest, and perhaps even help you, to look at the latest unemployment survey results.

Try to analyze these findings keeping in mind all we've discussed about gender and race. What may have caused these numbers? In what ways is a quantitative survey, which usually involves a large number or selected groups of people, limited? How do these results agree with or contradict what we have discussed in class? Don't forget the basic theories studied at the beginning of our time together.

Attached is the survey. Good luck with your finals. I'll look forward to reading your papers, and to those I don't see, enjoy your summer vacations.

THE EMPLOYMENT SITUATION
DECEMBER

Nonfarm employment increased by 167,000 in December, and the unemployment rate was unchanged at 4.5%, the Bureau of Labor Statistics of the U.S. Department of Labor reported today.

Job gains occurred in several service-providing industries, including professional and business services, healthcare, and food services. Average hourly earnings rose by 8%, or 0.5%, in December.

Unemployment (*Household Survey Data)*
The number of unemployed persons (6.8 million) was almost unchanged in December, and the unemployment rate was held at 4.5%.

So, in December, unemployment rates for the major worker groups – adult men (4.0%), adult women (3.9%), teenagers (15.2%), whites (4.0 %), blacks (8.4%), and Hispanics (4.9%) – showed little or no change. The unemployment rate for Asians was 2.4%, not seasonally adjusted.

Memo

Hi Joan,
Can you please send the email 're: SOCY101 Class' today as it will be useful to the students doing their finals now? It covers a lot of the data that they've been studying.
Thanks,
Alan

191. Why is the survey given to the class?
(A) It's meant to give them a break from finals.
(B) It's directly relevant to what they've studied.
(C) It gives a contradictory opinion of what they've studied.
(D) It's an extra assignment for their finals.

192. When was this email sent?
(A) at the beginning of the school year
(B) at around the end of the first semester
(C) at around the end of the school year
(D) during the summer vacation

193. How was this data accumulated?
(A) Many people were asked to answer certain questions.
(B) People searched databases on the internet.
(C) The data was extracted from basic sociological theories.
(D) Places of employment were observed.

194. What did NOT increase?
(A) nonfarm employment
(B) hourly earnings
(C) the unemployment rate
(D) jobs in healthcare

195. Which group has the smallest proportion of people without jobs?
(A) adult men
(B) adult women
(C) Hispanics
(D) teenagers

Questions 196–200 refer to the following letter, electronic ticket, and email.

Dear Mr Atkinson,

Thank you for giving Professional Travel Inc. the opportunity to make your travel arrangements for your forthcoming trip to Canada. Your electronic ticket for your flight is attached.

Please print it out and take it with you to the airport.

We hope that you are pleased with the air travel and the hotel accommodation that we have arranged for you. We encourage your comments, since that is the best means that we have for learning first-hand if the representations of quality that are made to us are accurate.

We hope that you have a pleasant and successful trip, and that you will afford us the opportunity to help you plan your next vacation or business trip.

Sincerely,
Maria Constantine
Professional Travel Inc.

e-ticket / voucher
Booking Number: 7050543
Invoice Number: 471016
Invoice Date: May 27

Zoom Airlines Inc
Suite 200, 380 Hunt Club Road
Ottawa, Ontario K1C 1V1
Canada
Tel: 613-235-9666
Fax: 613-231-7340

Flight Information

Flight Number	Departure Date	Departure Day	From	Departure Time	To	Arrival Time
ZA 523	20 June	Friday	London	15.05	Vancouver	16.10
ZA 722	29 June	Sunday	Vancouver	16.00	London	09.00

Seat Information: Business
Baggage allowance: 2 pieces Total weight 20kg
This ticket is not transferable/refundable to any other flight or person.
This receipt may be required at check-in and must be presented to Customs and Immigration if requested.

To: Paul Banks

Paul, I've just booked my work trip to Vancouver. I know you can't travel the same day as me, but I've got the accommodation sorted for us when you arrive the next day.

I've also booked us breakfast every day and there's a pool we can use. I didn't bother with the gym membership as we'll be too tired.

See you soon,
Aaron

196. What is the number of the invoice for the ticket?
(A) 471016
(B) 7050543
(C) 27-May
(D) K1C 1V1

197. Why does Professional Travel Inc. like receiving comments?
(A) to get an idea of how helpful their employees are
(B) because they enjoy positive feedback
(C) so they know if the hotels they recommend are good
(D) because this represents their quality

198. What does Mr Atkinson need to do with the ticket?
(A) print it out
(B) put it in a safe place
(C) pay for it
(D) transfer it to another person

199. What will Paul and Aaron probably not do?
(A) eat together
(B) go for a swim
(C) work out
(D) fly home together

200. How much baggage can Mr Atkinson take?
(A) two bags each weighing 20kg
(B) two bags each weighing 10kg
(C) four bags each weighing 5kg
(D) one bag weighing 25kg

Irregular Verbs

Infinitive	Simple Past	Past Participle
awake	awoke	awoken
be	was, were	been
bear	bore	borne
beat	beat	beaten
become	became	become
begin	began	begun
bend	bent	bent
beset	beset	beset
bet	bet	bet
bid	bid/bade	bid/bidden
bind	bound	bound
bite	bit	bitten
bleed	bled	bled
blow	blew	blown
break	broke	broken
breed	bred	bred
bring	brought	brought
broadcast	broadcast	broadcast
build	built	built
burn	burned/burnt	burned/burnt
burst	burst	burst
buy	bought	bought
cast	cast	cast
catch	caught	caught
choose	chose	chosen
cling	clung	clung
come	came	come
cost	cost	cost
creep	crept	crept
cut	cut	cut
deal	dealt	dealt
dig	dug	dug
dive	dived/dove	dived
do	did	done
draw	drew	drawn
dream	dreamed/dreamt	dreamed/dreamt
drive	drove	driven
drink	drank	drunk
eat	ate	eaten
fall	fell	fallen
feed	fed	fed
feel	felt	felt
fight	fought	fought
find	found	found
fit	fit	fit
flee	fled	fled
fling	flung	flung
fly	flew	flown
forbid	forbade	forbidden
forget	forgot	forgotten
forego (forgo)	forewent	foregone
forgive	forgave	forgiven
forsake	forsook	forsaken
freeze	froze	frozen
get	got	got/gotten
give	gave	given
go	went	gone

Infinitive	Simple Past	Past Participle
grind	ground	ground
grow	grew	grown
hang	hung	hung
hear	heard	heard
hide	hid	hidden
hit	hit	hit
hold	held	held
hurt	hurt	hurt
keep	kept	kept
kneel	knelt	knelt
knit	knit/knitted	knit/knitted
know	knew	known
lay	laid	laid
lead	led	led
leap	leaped/leapt	leaped/leapt
learn	learned/learnt	learned/learnt
leave	left	left
lend	lent	lent
let	let	let
lie	lay	lain
light	lighted/lit	lighted/lit
lose	lost	lost
make	made	made
mean	meant	meant
meet	met	met
misspell	misspelled/misspelt	misspelled/misspelt
mistake	mistook	mistaken
mow	mowed	mowed/mown
overcome	overcame	overcome
overdo	overdid	overdone
overtake	overtook	overtaken
overthrow	overthrew	overthrown
pay	paid	paid
plead	pleaded/pled	pleaded/pled
prove	proved	proved/proven
put	put	put
quit	quit/quitted	quit/quitted
read	read	read
rid	rid/ridded	rid
ride	rode	ridden
ring	rang	rung
rise	rose	risen
run	ran	run
saw	sawed	sawed/sawn
say	said	said
see	saw	seen
seek	sought	sought
sell	sold	sold
send	sent	sent
set	set	set
sew	sewed	sewed/sewn
shake	shook	shaken
shave	shaved	shaved/shaven
shear	sheared	shorn
shed	shed	shed
shine	shone	shone
shoe	shoed	shoed/shod
shoot	shot	shot

Infinitive	Simple Past	Past Participle
show	showed	showed/shown
shrink	shrank	shrunk
shut	shut	shut
sing	sang	sung
sink	sank	sunk
sit	sat	sat
sleep	slept	slept
slay	slew	slain
slide	slid	slid
sling	slung	slung
slit	slit	slit
smite	smote	smitten
sow	sowed	sowed/sown
speak	spoke	spoken
speed	sped/speeded	sped
spend	spent	spent
spill	spilled/spilt	spilled/spilt
spin	spun	spun
spit	spit/spat	spit
split	split	split
spread	spread	spread
spring	sprang/sprung	sprung
stand	stood	stood
steal	stole	stolen
stick	stuck	stuck
stingstink	stungstank	stungstunk
stride	strode	stridden
strike	struck	struck
string	strung	strung
strive	strove	striven
swear	swore	sworn
sweep	swept	swept
swell	swelled	swelled/swollen
swim	swam	swum
swing	swung	swung
take	took	taken
teach	taught	taught
tear	tore	torn
tell	told	told
think	thought	thought
thrive	thrived/throve	thrived
throw	threw	thrown
thrust	thrust	thrust
tread	trod	trodden
understand	understood	understood
uphold	upheld	upheld
upset	upset	upset
wake	woke	woken
wear	wore	worn
weave	weaved/wove	weaved/woven
wed	wed	wed
weep	wept	wept
wind	wound	wound
win	won	won
withhold	withheld	withheld
withstand	withstood	withstood
wring	wrung	wrung
write	wrote	written

TEST 1

In this section of the test, you will have the chance to show how well you understand spoken English. There are four parts to this section, with special directions for each part.

Part 1

Directions: For each question, you will see a picture and you will hear four short statements. The statements will be spoken just one time. They will not be printed in your test book so you must listen carefully to understand what the speaker says. When you hear the four statements, look at the picture and choose the statement that best describes what you see in the picture. Choose the best answer (A), (B), (C), or (D).

EXAMPLE:
Now listen to the four statements. You will hear:
A He is on the phone.
B She is driving the car.
C She is typing on the computer.
D He is sitting next to her.
Statement (D) best describes what you see in the picture. Therefore, you should choose answer (D).

1. (A) A woman is giving birth.
(B) A woman is touching her own stomach.
(C) A woman is going to have a baby.
(D) A pregnant woman is wearing sleeves.
2. (A) There are candles centered on the table.
(B) They are being served food.
(C) They are on unusual seats.
(D) They are in a bathroom.
3. (A) They are pushing babies in strollers.
(B) The babies are being carried.
(C) They are walking on a sidewalk.
(D) They are on a busy street.
4. (A) He is gesturing.
(B) She has something on her lap.
(C) They are sitting next to each other.
(D) He is listening to her.
5. (A) He is dressed casually.
(B) She is holding the microphone.
(C) She is dressed formally.
(D) She is addressing him.
6. (A) The stepladder is not in use.
(B) They are kneeling.
(C) They are polishing a cabinet.
(D) There is a hammer on the ground.

Part 2

Directions: In this part of the test, you will hear a question or statement spoken in English, followed by three responses, also spoken in English. The question or statement and the responses will be spoken just one time. They will not be printed in your test book, so you must listen carefully. You are to choose the best response to each question or statement. Now listen to a sample question. You will hear:
Man: Why are you late?
Woman: A. I hope I won't be.
B. My car broke down.
C. He always is.
The best response is choice (B): "My car broke down". Therefore, you should choose (B).

7. M: What time is your flight?
W: A. Next week.
B. Four in the morning.
C. I'm usually on time.
8. W: Where are you going?
M: A. In about 10 minutes.
B. With John and Sally.
C. To the shops.
9. M: Who lives in that house?
W: A. Yes, I do.
B. It has three bedrooms.
C. My brother, Billy.
10. W: What's wrong with the telephone?
M: A. It doesn't seem to be working.
B. There's a message for you.
C. I'll call you later.
11. M: Did you enjoy the film?
W: A. I'm sure we will.
B. Sometimes I do.
C. Very much.
12. W: What's the name of the cafe you go to?
M: A. Yes, that's the one.
B. It's called the Black Cat.
C. It's not that far.
13. M: When is Brian's birthday?
W: A. Is it really?
B. Here's a present for you.
C. Sometime next week.
14. W: Who can type this letter for me?
M: A. I have a stamp here.
B. Would you like some paper?
C. I can do it when I finish this report.
15. M: Will the meeting be held in the director's office?
W: A. That's what the memo said.
B. No, in about an hour's time.
C. It's the first street on the left.
16. W: You're Mrs Brown's new assistant, aren't you?
M: A. I don't need any help, thank you.
B. Of course I can assist you.
C. No, I work for Mr Davis.
17. M: Will you take a picture of us?
W: A. I didn't take it.
B. Certainly!
C. I can't draw to save my life.
18. W: Do you want the steak or the chicken?
M: A. It's not in the kitchen.
B. I'll have steak or beer.
C. They both sound good.
19. M: Do you know why David is late?
W: A. He's late as usual.
B. Almost an hour.
C. Maybe he missed the bus.
20. W: Are you ready to order now, sir?
M: A. Just give me a minute.
B. I'll happily take your order.
C. That's a good choice.
21. M: Are there any messages for me?
W: A. I didn't say anything.
B. Yes, what is it?
C. One from the bank.
22. W: Would you like to join us for a game of tennis?
M: A. We'd be delighted.
B. We joined last week.
C. That was a great game.
23. M: How long have you lived at your present home?
W: A. I've been looking for ages.
B. Ever since I was a child.
C. You shouldn't have bought me a present.
24. W: That's Ben's briefcase, isn't it?
M: A. It sure is.
B. It's not that brief.
C. If you insist.
25. M: Is this blue coat on sale?
W: A. I've got a blue coat.
B. I don't like sailing.
C. Yes, it's half-price.
26. W: Who is the new secretary?
M: A. In the main office.
B. Yes, she's very efficient.
C. Her name is Janet Swinton.
27. M: Is the food prepared?
W: A. I'm ready.
B. Yes, it's on the table.
C. Unfortunately, it's broken.

28. W: How about going to the theater for a treat?
M: A. The doctor said the treatment was successful.
B. It's just next to the hospital.
C. That's a great idea.

29. M: Did you finish the report yet?
W: A. I don't like watching the news.
B. Not quite.
C. She's a good reporter.

30. W: Are you hungry?
M: A. Only because you annoyed me.
B. I'm starving.
C. I'm not in a hurry.

31. M: Do you have a cold?
W: A. It was freezing today.
B. He's not that old.
C. I've had one for a few days.

Part 3

Directions: You will hear some conversations between two or more people. You will be asked to answer three questions about what the speakers say in each conversation. Select the best response to each question and mark the letter (A), (B), (C), or (D) on your answer sheet. The conversations will not be printed in your test book and will be spoken only one time.

Questions 32 through 34 refer to the following conversation:
W: Hi, Michael, can I have a word?
M: Certainly, Megan. Come in. How is preparation for the conference going?
W: Well, that's what I wanted to speak to you about.
M: No problems I hope ...
W: No, no real problems. But I've just finished writing my presentation, and really I have no idea if it's at the right level for the audience. I was wondering, since you've been to a lot of these conferences, if you could listen to my presentation and tell me what you think?
M: Yes, of course. However, I have a deadline on Thursday and my schedule's pretty full ... When's your conference?
W: The 10th.
M: Oh, OK! You have a bit of time then. How about Friday the 5th, in the morning?
W: That would be great, thanks.

32. How does Megan feel about the presentation she will give?
33. What is true about Megan?
34. What will happen on Friday the 5th?

Questions 35 through 37 refer to the following conversation:
M: Hello, can I help you?
W: Yes, I'm not sure if I'm in the right place, but I'm looking for some information on your organization. You see, I've just graduated and I'd like to get involved doing some voluntary work with disabled children this summer. I have my CV. Am I in the right office?
M: No, I'm afraid you want to talk to Anna in 261 B. She's not in this afternoon, though. She only works from 9 a.m. to 1 p.m. each day.
W: Oh.
M: But do come back tomorrow if you can; I know she's always looking for volunteers.

35. What is the woman trying to do?
36. What does the woman need to do next?
37. How could the man be best described?

Questions 38 through 40 refer to the following conversation:
W: Did you manage to book our flights?
M: Yes, this morning. We'll leave at 18.45 on Thursday and arrive at 22.10 in Berlin. Then we'll return ...
W: Wait a minute, didn't Elsie tell you that I'm not available on Thursday evening? I have to work until 8 p.m.! I said specifically that I need to go Friday morning. We don't have to be there till afternoon, after all!
M: Uh, no. I didn't hear anything about this.
W: Great! What are we going to do now?
M: Well, I just have to call back and change your ticket, I guess.

38. How does the woman feel?
39. Why did the man make a mistake?
40. Why couldn't the woman go on Thursday evening?

Questions 41 through 43 refer to the following conversation:
M: Lovely day, isn't it?
W1: It certainly is. It's just a shame we're stuck in here behind computers!
W2: Couldn't agree more.
M: You can say that again! Any exciting plans for the weekend?
W1: Yes, Todd and I wanna take the kids to the seaside. I hope the weather holds up.
M: Hmm, what a shame we can't take "sun days"; you know, like sick days! One day a month, in cases of exceptional weather, to maintain our mental health and well-being!
W1: Oh, you know what our manager would have to say about that!
W2: We sure do.

41. What would the first woman like to be doing on the weekend?
42. What is the tone of the man's words?
43. What is the relationship between the three speakers?

Questions 44 through 46 refer to the following conversation:
M: Hello, Ms Johnson. Do you have a minute?
W: What is it, Tim?
M: Well, you know we have this environmental report that needs finishing by Monday ...
W: I certainly don't know how I'd forget about that!
M: Yes, well, I wanted to let you know that there's no way I'm gonna finish my section.
W: Why's that?
M: It's just not realistically possible – lots of problems in the data.
W: Yes, most of us are struggling. I guess I'll have to try to arrange an extension. Thanks for letting me know anyway.

44. Why does the woman say, "Yes, most of us are struggling."?
45. What was the purpose of the man's conversation with Ms Johnson?
46. What is the relationship between the man and Ms Johnson?

Questions 47 through 49 refer to the following conversation:
W: Have you heard? Laura got a job offer from a university in Australia.
M: Really? That was quite a good position, wasn't it? Do you think she'll take it?
W: I don't know. I think she might. When I met with her for coffee and she told me the news, her eyes were sparkling and she had a huge smile! She was talking mostly about the disadvantages, though.
M: What a hard decision! Australia is very far away. She would miss her family and friends.
W: Yes, but I think she would love the adventure, though.

47. What does the woman imply when she says, "Her eyes were sparkling and she had a huge smile!"?
48. What does the woman think Laura will do?
49. Why does the man think it would be hard for Laura to decide to take the job?

Questions 50 through 52 refer to the following conversation:
M: So, did you buy the car in the end?
W: Emm, no, actually.
M: You didn't? You were so excited about it last week!
W: Yes, that car was a super deal and I loved the color, but I've decided that I don't need a car. What would I be using it for? Really, only trips on the weekend. I take the Underground to work and that's fine. I could just rent a car for the weekend sometimes and it would come out a lot cheaper.

M: Yes, but I think if you have to rent a car, you would be much less likely to go. If the car is sitting there waiting, you're almost obliged to go on a trip!

50. How did the man feel when he heard about the woman's decision?
51. How often does the woman think she would use the car?
52. What does the man think is the problem with renting a car?

Questions 53 through 55 refer to the following conversation:
W1: I don't know what to do about my new office mate. She sits next to me all day and never says a word to me. It makes me really uncomfortable.
M: Have you tried to talk to her?
W1: Yes, at first I always said hello and tried to chat a little, and she responded politely, but if I don't speak first, she acts like she doesn't even see me!
W2: She sounds a bit stuck-up to me.
M: Maybe she's shy. I'd just keep trying to be friendly.
W1: But what if it bothers her?
M: Why don't you ask if it bothers her?
W2: You've got nothing to lose, have you?

53. How is the woman feeling?
54. Why is the woman unhappy with her office mate?
55. How does the man think the woman should be?

Questions 56 through 58 refer to the following conversation:
M: Excuse me ... Excuse me!
W: Yes, can I help you, sir?
M: I hope so. There's a bit of a problem with my order. I specifically asked for a salad without tomatoes because I really can't stand them, and now, here is my side salad with tomatoes in it. OK, it's not the end of the world if I don't eat it because at least I've got the steak and chips, but it's just that I specifically asked ...
W: Oh, I'm very sorry. I guess the chef didn't notice my note. Just a moment and I'll bring another.

56. What food does the man not like?
57. If the man doesn't eat his salad, what will happen?
58. How can the woman be described?

Questions 59 through 61 refer to the following conversation:
W: Hi, I just wanted to let you know that the proposal went really well. We've got the contract and we're doing the park!
M: That's fantastic! It was a fun space to work with.
W: Your design was really original and fun, particularly the children's play area. So, thanks for all your hard work.
M: I'm glad they liked it. When do they want us to start?
W: As soon as possible, really. I told them we were available to start in April. We need to find some people to do the landscaping and the construction.

59. What is the man's job?
60. What was the man's attitude towards his work?
61. Why is the woman speaking to the man?

Questions 62 through 64 refer to the following conversation:
M: Have you had many sales this week?
W: It's been very slow. I'm still waiting for my first buyer. I sold two last week, and I had a couple that were very interested in a house in town. I need to sell three more by the end of the month to reach my target.
M: I don't know what to do with myself all day. This economic depression is stopping people from buying. People seem to be reluctant to even look at the moment. I wish they'd be a bit braver and buy while the prices are down.
W: I'm going to pop out for a bite to eat!
M: Are you going to the cafe or the canteen?
W: I thought I'd go to the store as I left my sandwiches in the fridge at home again.

62. Look at the graphic. Who is currently interested in buying some property?
63. How does the man feel?
64. Where is the woman going now?

Questions 65 through 67 refer to the following conversation:
M: Did you get the memo about Tuesday's meeting?
W: The one about the Parson Project in the morning?
M: No, that's for the administration, I mean the Finance Department. The design meeting is in the afternoon.
W: I guess management will be their usual annoying selves. They never contribute anything useful to the meetings.
M: I'm tired of these meetings. They should just let us get on with the job. I can't wait to really get involved with the main project, but they keep delaying everything.

65. Which department do the speakers work in?
66. What is the woman's attitude towards the managers?
67. How does the man feel?

Questions 68 through 70 refer to the following conversation:
M1: So, are you going to buy that house?
W: We decided against it in the end, after a lot of indecision.
M1: I thought it was your dream home.
W: I got carried away with the village, but the property itself wasn't really what we need as a family. The garden was acceptable, although it could have been a bit bigger, and the view was nothing special.
M2: Yeah, I need a big garden to grow vegetables.
W: Absolutely.
M1: I know you have a budget that you can't go over, so maybe you need to rethink what is really important to you. That house obviously wasn't right despite the great location.
M2: Bill has a point there, Jane. We can't go over 200,000.

68. How did the first man feel when he heard about the woman's decision?
69. Look at the graphic. Which property are they discussing?
70. What does Bill think the woman should do?

Part 4

Directions: You will hear some talks given by a single speaker. You will be asked to answer three questions about what the speaker says in each talk. Select the best response to each question and mark the letter (A), (B), (C), or (D) on your answer sheet. The talks will not be printed in your test book and will be spoken only one time.

Questions 71 through 73 refer to the following speech:
It is with great pleasure that I welcome you to this special opening ceremony today. Today is the result of over five years' planning and hard work as we finally open this magnificent building. Of course, we must thank the Bradford family, who have given their wonderful art collection to the city. You will see many fine examples of classical and modern art on the walls around you. The Bradford family made their fortune making and selling beautiful clothes but, luckily for us, they spent a lot of their money on works of art. And now, ladies and gentlemen, please welcome Alan Bradford, the great-grandson of the late Charles Bradford, who will officially open the building and make a little speech himself.

71. What is the building?
72. What were the Bradford family?
73. Who is Charles Bradford?

Questions 74 through 76 refer to the following announcement:
Your attention, please. Would all passengers for the 11.15 to Atlanta please proceed to platform six as the train now standing at platform four is the 10.50 to Washington? This change of platform is due to a problem with the signals. The 11.15 to Atlanta will be delayed by 15 minutes and will not be leaving until 11.30. This is the express train and so will not stop en route. For the slow train to Atlanta, please board the train now standing at platform seven. This will be departing at 11.40 from platform seven. Thank you.

74. What has affected the 10.50 train to Washington?

75. Look at the graphic. Which one of these trains is an express one?
76. Which platform will the Washington train leave from?

Questions 77 through 79 refer to the following speech:
Hello, my name is John. I'll be serving your table tonight. Today we have some delicious specials. We have grilled salmon with a honey glaze; roast chicken; mixed grill; or steak and pepper. We also have a fine selection of salad and vegetables. I'll come around later with the dessert trolley as there are far too many tasty things to mention.

77. Who is talking?
78. How many specials are there to choose from?
79. What does he not tell them about immediately?

Questions 80 through 82 refer to the following talk:
This is "The Sky at Night". Today, we have the acclaimed astronomer Mervyn Skylark. Mervyn is going to talk to us about the growing problem of light pollution in our cities. Five out of the 12 signs of the zodiac have already been removed from view by light pollution, and campaigners are trying to persuade governments to do something to change this problem. The amount of light pouring out into the night sky has increased by a quarter in the past 10 years, and only 11 per cent of the country is free of light pollution. Now over to our expert, Mervyn, but first a little music.

80. Who is the talk directed at?
81. By what percentage has light pollution increased over the last 10 years?
82. What is the next thing the listeners will hear?

Questions 83 through 85 refer to the following speech:
Good evening, ladies and gentlemen, and may I welcome you to the Astoria Theatre. Tonight's film, "The Longest Day", is the third in this week's series of 12 films about human relationships. This is the second time we've run a film series, and I'm sure it will be as popular as the first one. "The Longest Day" is a moving film about a father's struggle to deal with his son's illness. For 24 hours, the father doesn't know if his son will live or die. The film, which runs for 120 minutes, will break even the hardest heart. After the film, we invite you to a cheese and wine reception and you will have the chance to talk to both the director and some of the actors.

83. How many films will be shown this week?
84. Why does the speaker say, "The film will break even the hardest heart."?
85. What will happen after the film?

Questions 86 through 88 refer to the following announcement:
Attention, shoppers! Today we have all sorts of bargains and special offers to tell you about. Firstly, on the ground floor, KidsWorld is giving away free toys to any child who persuades their mom or dad to purchase something from the store. On the top floor, The Coffee Place has a special offer of a free cake with each drink purchased. Don't forget the cafes close at 5 p.m., so make sure you stop for a break before then. Tonight's late-night shopping finishes at 8 p.m., so only four more hours to buy those final purchases. Happy shopping!

86. Why does the speaker say, "Attention, shoppers!"?
87. Where can you get something free to eat?
88. What time is it now?

Questions 89 through 91 refer to the following announcement:
Good morning, and welcome aboard Skybird International Flight 362 from London to Cape Town, with intermediate stops in Paris and Cairo. We will be departing in 10 minutes. Please check that your seat belt is fastened, and we urge you to pay attention to the safety instructions. Our anticipated flying time to Paris is one hour, 10 minutes, and then we will be proceeding to Cairo, where we are due to land at 16.00 hours. On behalf of the captain and the rest of the crew, we wish you a safe and pleasant flight.

89. Where are they?
90. Who is speaking?
91. Look at the graphic. What time are they departing from London?

Questions 92 through 94 refer to the following directions:
OK, sir. I think I understand what the problem is with your computer. I'll try to talk you through how to fix the problem over the phone, but if that doesn't work, you'll have to take the computer in to our nearest service center. OK, first, are you connected to the internet? Good, OK, make sure all your other programs are closed. Now, find the "My computer icon" and double-click on it. In this box, find a place called "programs" and double-click on that. Now, you should see that you have a list of all the programs on your computer ...

92. What is the problem?
93. The man speaking is
94. What should be done first?

Questions 95 through 97 refer to the following news report:
Good morning, this is the 9 o'clock business news! The dollar has edged towards seven-week lows against both the yen and the euro because of fears about poor US retail sales and banking results. Investment banks have already predicted that the US economy will fall into recession in two years' time, and analysts are also nervously awaiting the release of retail sales data for December. As consumer spending accounts for two-thirds of the US economy, the figure may indicate whether the fears are correct. In December, the US Federal Reserve cut the interest rates for the third time as it tried to help steer the world's largest economy through the continuing housing slump.

95. Who is most likely speaking?
96. What is predicted to happen in two years' time?
97. What accounts for two-thirds of the US economy?

Questions 98 through 100 refer to the following speech:
I want to extend a warm welcome to all our delegates at our third annual renewable energy conference! And it's great to see so many familiar faces from last year. First of all, I want to make sure that you've all registered. If you haven't registered yet, please go to our registration table in the lobby of the hotel. You will receive the conference schedule, among other things. Next, I want to point out that the presentations begin promptly at 9 a.m. tomorrow morning, and our first presentation should be very interesting, so I would encourage all of you to make the effort to get up! It will be worth your while! And don't forget breakfast is served starting at 7 a.m.

98. Who is being spoken to?
99. How many times has this conference taken place before?
100. What happens at 9 a.m. tomorrow?

That is the end of the test.

TEST 2

In this section of the test, you will have the chance to show how well you understand spoken English. There are four parts to this section, with special directions for each part.

Part 1

Directions: For each question, you will see a picture and you will hear four short statements. The statements will be spoken just one time. They will not be printed in your test book so you must listen carefully to understand what the speaker says. When you hear the four statements, look at the picture and choose the statement that best describes what you see in the picture. Choose the best answer (A), (B), (C), or (D).

Audio Script

EXAMPLE:
Now listen to the four statements. You will hear:
(A) He is on the phone.
(B) She is driving the car.
(C) She is typing on the computer.
(D) He is sitting next to her.
Statement (D) best describes what you see in the picture. Therefore, you should choose answer (D).

1. (A) They are applauding the speaker.
(B) The speaker is gesturing with her hands.
(C) The speaker is behind the podium.
(D) They are looking away from the speaker.
2. (A) The plane is taking off.
(B) They are seated in an airplane.
(C) The passengers are disembarking.
(D) They are boarding from outside.
3. (A) Both men are wearing ties.
(B) The woman speaking is wearing glasses.
(C) All the women are crossing their legs.
(D) Two people are speaking at once.
4. (A) Papers are scattered on the table.
(B) They are seated across from each other.
(C) They are all looking at the same document.
(D) Notebooks are in a pile on the table.
5. (A) He is saluting a flag.
(B) He has something strapped on his shoulder.
(C) She is not pleased with him.
(D) She is avoiding eye contact.
6. (A) One man is wearing jeans.
(B) The woman is holding her bag.
(C) The man wearing a vest has a beard.
(D) The woman doesn't have a name tag.

Part 2

Directions: In this part of the test, you will hear a question or statement spoken in English, followed by three responses, also spoken in English. The question or statement and the responses will be spoken just one time. They will not be printed in your test book, so you must listen carefully. You are to choose the best response to each question or statement. Now listen to a sample question. You will hear:
Man: Why are you late?
Woman: (A) I hope I won't be.
(B) My car broke down.
(C) He always is.

The best response is choice B: "My car broke down". Therefore, you should choose B.

7. M: What time does your plane leave?
W: A. It wasn't on time.
B. I hope it does.
C. An hour after yours.
8. W: What kind of movies do you like to watch?
M: A. I hire them from the video store.
B. I prefer thrillers.
C. I went to the movies last week.
9. M: How well can Anne play tennis?
W: A. She plays three times a week.
B. At the local tennis club.
C. She's really good.
10. W: How did you spot the mistake?
M: A. It won't happen again, I promise.
B. It wasn't an important one.
C. By going through everything really carefully.
11. M: How old is your son?
W: A. He's six but he looks older.
B. He's really quite tall.
C. He takes after his father.
12. W: How about going out for lunch on Sunday?
M: A. Chicken and salad.
B. It was very tasty, thanks.
C. Sorry, I'm already doing something on Sunday.
13. M: What does John do for a living?
W: A. He lives in Chicago.
B. He's an engineer.
C. He has a big townhouse.
14. W: Did anyone call while I was out?
M: A. I didn't call you.
B. Not even one person.
C. I'll call you in a minute.
15. M: Does anyone know whose keys these are?
W: A. They look like Mike's.
B. The lock is broken.
C. I'll get some new keys cut.
16. W: I've written a song. Would you like to hear it?
M: A. At a concert?
B. Why not?
C. He's a good singer.
17. M: Would you mind if I left an hour early?
W: A. If you really need to.
B. I'm always early.
C. It will take an hour to get there.
18. W: Should I put the fruit in paper or plastic bags?
M: A. Paper, please.
B. Bags are better than boxes.
C. Yes, you should.
19. M: Why is Peter late?
W: A. He wasn't late.
B. Probably because of the bus strike.
C. Almost two hours now.
20. W: Shall I turn on the air-conditioning?
M: A. No, it shouldn't be.
B. Yes, it is.
C. Good idea.
21. M: Will that be to eat in or take away?
W: A. Please take it away immediately.
B. What do you think?
C. We'll eat it here.
22. W: Do you know when the gallery opens?
M: A. Of course it is.
B. At nine o'clock.
C. It's in the next street.
23. M: What's the matter with Cherie?
W: A. I didn't say I was angry with her.
B. Her boyfriend left her.
C. She's over there.
24. W: Can you tell me where to catch the bus?
M: A. At 2.30.
B. To the train station.
C. Just outside the museum.
25. M: How did you get to school today?
W: A. I'm doing fine, thanks.
B. By bike.
C. I have to study a lot.
26. W: How long has he worked for that company?
M: A. Only since last May.
B. He'll be finished in one hour.
C. In the Accounts Department.
27. M: Can I pay by check?
W: A. I'll pay by credit card.
B. Here's your change.
C. We only take cash.
28. W: How about going for a run?
M: A. Shall we run in the park?
B. It's too far to run.
C. I've run lots of races.
29. M: What time do you usually have dinner?
W: A. It's too late to eat.
B. It depends how late I get home from work.
C. I've already eaten.
30. W: What's Susan like?
M: A. I'd like to meet her.
B. She liked the present.
C. She's very considerate.
31. M: Where was the passport found?
W: A. I've got it in my bag.
B. On the floor, under a chair.
C. From the Passport Office.

Part 3

Directions: You will hear some conversations between two or more people. You will be asked to answer three questions about what the speakers say in each conversation. Select the best response to each question and mark the letter (A), (B), (C), or (D) on your answer sheet. The conversations will not be printed in your test book and will be spoken only one time.

Questions 32 through 34 refer to this conversation:
W: Hi! I'm sorry I'm late. The traffic on 35E was impossible.
M: Really? But it's not even rush hour.
W: I know, but it's summertime and there's a lot of construction.
M: Well, anyway, I suppose we shouldn't waste any more time. We've got a lot of work today before the big presentation tomorrow.
W: Oh, I cannot wait until it is all over and done with. I have such a fear of public speaking.
M: What's there to be afraid of? You know the material better than anyone in the class.
W: It's all mental; it has nothing to do with the material. But whenever I stand up in front of other people, I start trembling. My mouth goes dry, I start stuttering, and I also fidget with my hands.
M: Now you're making me nervous. We'd better practice a lot. Certainly the content is more important than delivery, but people need to understand what you are saying!
W: OK, let's finish putting together the last of the pages for the PowerPoint presentation, and then we'll rehearse until it's perfect. If I say the presentation enough times, I think the words will flow easier tomorrow.
M: OK, let's get cracking.

32. What is the reason for the traffic on 35E?
33. What is at fault for the woman's nervousness?
34. What, according to the man, is the most important part of the presentation?

Questions 35 through 37 refer to this conversation:
M: Have either of you seen the Knight file? It was on my desk this morning, and now it is nowhere to be found.
W1: I think Meredith said she wanted to look it over before the meeting with the administrators tonight.
M: Well, where is Meredith? I haven't seen her for a while now.
W2: I think she's out for a few hours. She said something about meetings at the other office. I'm not sure, to tell you the truth.
M: I'll have to call her on her cell, then. I really need that file. I need to have it memorized by the meeting tonight, and I haven't even glanced at it yet.
W2: OK, call her. But be warned, she always turns her phone off when she is in meetings.
M: Oh, no. Well, I suppose it's my own fault for saving it until the very last moment. She probably assumed that I had already looked at it, considering it's been in my possession for the last three days.
W1: So what are you going to do if you don't get a chance to read it?
M: Wing it, I guess. And let Meredith do most of the talking.

35. Why does the man want to find Meredith?
36. What is the man upset about?
37. What does the man imply he will do at the meeting tonight?

Questions 38 through 40 refer to this conversation:
W: How did the interview go? Do you feel confident?
M: I honestly have no idea what to think about the interview.
W: What do you mean?
M: I was extremely nervous. My palms were sweaty and I stuttered on almost every question.
W: You don't strike me as the type of person who gets flustered.
M: I usually don't! But this man was so intimidating. He had such an arrogant presence to him. After the question, he leaned back in his chair and crossed his arms, as if he had just dared me to answer a question and expected me to fail.
W: I'm sure that was just his strategy. He probably wanted to observe how you handled pressure.
M: It really threw me off guard. I really wish I could have come off as more confident.
W: Well, don't forget that the decision is not entirely dependent on the interview. You have an outstanding academic record, you did an impeccable job on your application, and I have no doubt that your references will sing your praises to them as well.

38. What effect did the interviewer have on the man?
39. What, besides the interview, could help the man get the job?
40. What is the woman's opinion?

Questions 41 through 43 refer to this conversation:
M: Here it is. Carousel A. And it says right here on the monitor that this has the luggage for Flight 532 arriving from New York.
W1: It sure is crowded here. We're going to have to really push and shove to get to our luggage.
M: Well, we don't have to be at the convention center for another three hours, and both the hotel and the center are only minutes away from the airport. What do you say we go and get some coffee over at that coffee stand in the corner?
W2: That's a good idea. We can let the crowd die out a little bit and then come claim our luggage. Plus, I'm falling asleep! I could really use a caffeine kick!
M: Let's go then. My treat.
W1: You don't have to do that. Let us get it.
M: No, I insist. Consider it a small thank you for letting me ride with you to the airport this morning.
W1: OK, but we'll get the coffee on the way back.
M: Deal.

41. Where are the three individuals?
42. Why does the woman say, "Plus, I'm falling asleep!"?
43. Why does he want to pay for the coffee?

Questions 44 through 46 refer to this conversation:
W: Excuse me. Is this Dr John Evans' office?
M: It sure is. Do you have an appointment?
W: No, actually. His name was given to me by a colleague. I've been suffering from insomnia for the last few months. I've gone to M.D.s and taken herbs and nothing seems to work. I thought a psychologist might help me work through the stress that is causing the insomnia.
M: That sounds like a reasonable solution to me. Now, Dr Evans is booked every day, so I'm afraid you can't see him without an appointment.
W: I figured that much. I just came to the actual office instead of calling because I was in the area. Can I make an appointment with you, then?
M: Definitely. We'll schedule you first for a half-hour consultation. After that consultation, Dr Evans will suggest how often you should come and we'll schedule accordingly.
W: That sounds good. When can I get an appointment?
M: Usually he's booked for weeks straight. But fortunately for you, he just had a cancellation for this Friday at 2. Can you make it?
W: I'll be there.

44. Who referred the woman to Dr Evans?
45. Why does the woman want to be Dr Evans's patient?
46. Look at the graphic. What is the woman's name?

Questions 47 through 49 refer to this conversation:
M: Are you just getting back from work now? It's late.
W: I know. I had the greatest day, though.
M: You are the only person I know who comes back from 14 hours of work and calls it a great day.
W: Well, this new job is very exciting for me. It's the first time I'm doing something I actually love and I am talented at.
M: So, why was it such a great day?
W: My boss let me sit in on a meeting with the Calvin Klein designer, which I take as a sign that she is preparing me to have more responsibilities in the future.
M: I think that is a safe assumption.

W: Also, I told her I liked a certain design and she ordered a ton of it.
M: It sounds like you are really earning the respect of your boss, and quickly too! You have accomplished a lot in just two months on the job.

47. According to the man, what is unique about the woman?
48. What does going to the Calvin Klein meeting probably mean for the woman?
49. Why did the boss order a lot of a particular design?

Questions 50 through 52 refer to this conversation:
W: Are you leaving for home already, Ed? It's only 3.30.
M: I know. But I've been here since 7.
W: Why the sudden change of schedule? I've never known you to be an early bird.
M: I'm definitely not, and I am somewhat sleep-deprived. But my son is in the state soccer tournament and I can't miss any of his games.
W: You are such a dedicated father. And an employee at that! I'm not nearly as efficient as you are in the office. But the first thing I do when I come home is take a nap. I don't know how you have the energy to work full-time and have a family.
M: Well, I wasn't up to it at your age, that's for sure. This is only your first year on the job. It takes a while to get a rhythm. Once you're settled here, you'll find you'll have more energy for other aspects of your life, I promise! OK, I better go. I can't miss kick-off!
W: Have fun and good luck to your son!

50. Why is it acceptable for Ed to leave at 3.30?
51. What does the woman admire about the man?
52. How does the man reassure the woman?

Questions 53 through 55 refer to this conversation:
W: Adam, hi! What are you doing here?
M: Since you weren't answering any of your calls, I thought I'd make a home visit.
W: I know, I'm sorry. I know you are looking for this week's column, and I know I'm past deadline ... It's just that I had some family things come up this week and I'm a little behind schedule.
M: Jenny, you are always past deadline. And although, as your editor, that used to stress me out a lot, I've grown accustomed to it the last few years.
W: Well, then what is this about? Is something wrong?
M: Well, a publishing company contacted me a week ago with an interest in turning your columns into a book. I promised to set up a meeting between you and them by the end of the week, but then again, I didn't expect you to be avoiding my calls for seven days straight.
W: Are you serious?!
M: Yes, I'm serious, but they are starting to think that YOU are not serious. I've set up a meeting for today at four. Can you make it?
W: Of course!

53. What has the man gotten used to?
54. What does the publishing company want to meet with the woman about?
55. Why does the woman say, "Are you serious?!"?

Questions 56 through 58 refer to this conversation:
M: As I said over the phone, I've been an accountant for the last 10 years and have recently quit my job. I want to find a career that I am passionate about.
W: And what provoked your interest in advertising?
M: Well, there's still a lot for me to learn about the field, but it seems to grant me the opportunity to exercise both my creativity and my intelligence.
W: That is certainly true. And there is actually an opening at the agency.
M: Honestly? What position is it?
W: It's an unpaid internship. It will allow you to dabble in the various aspects of the advertising world so you can find a specific area that suits you best. Also, it will allow you to develop a strong portfolio.
M: But did you say unpaid?
W: Well, yes. Remember, you are starting a new career so you're going to have to start at the bottom and work your way up. It will be years until you make what you were making at your old job.

56. Why does the man want to be in advertising?
57. According to the woman, why should he get the job at the agency?
58. Look at the graphic. Which job would the man be most interested in and suitable for?

Questions 59 through 61 refer to this conversation:
M: Do you think James will get the promotion?
W: He definitely has a good chance and certainly deserves it. But remember, Paul is the boss's nephew and he is also up for the job.
M: But Cindy's a fair boss. She would never promote someone who was less qualified just because they were family.
W: I don't think she would do it consciously, but it may play some role in her decision-making. I mean, it's not like Paul is completely unqualified for the position. If Paul and James are neck and neck for the position, Paul certainly has the edge.
M: Well, James will just be wrecked if he doesn't get it. He's been working so hard.
W: Let's just hope for the best.

59. What might hinder James's chance at the job?
60. What does the woman think about Paul?
61. What does the man know about Paul?

Questions 62 through 64 refer to the following conversation:
W: Why is John in such a bad mood? Didn't he get his promotion?
M: No, it's not that. The printer has broken on his computer and he needs a report for this morning's meeting with the accountant.
W: Why didn't he use mine? I can't believe how silly you two are at times.
M: There's no point me saying anything, he's still in a mood about the contract that I beat him to.
W: Well, you know that I think you are both being very immature about that. If you two don't pull your socks up, you'll annoy our boss and neither of you will get a promotion.

62. What is wrong with John?
63. What does the woman think about the men's behavior?
64. What is the relationship between the man and the woman?

Questions 65 through 67 refer to the following conversation:
M: Hi, good news, we got the contract!
W1: That's fantastic. I think most of the credit goes to you, though, as you really made it look good with your computer images.
W2: Absolutely, I agree with Sally.
M: Yes, but you two did the designs, so you are truly the creative ones. Let's hope that we can really stick to the budget now, because I was stretching the truth a bit on costs. I'm not very good with finances at the best of times.
W1: Am I supposed to be impressed by that? You may have put the whole project at risk. How could you do such a thing?
W2: I can't believe you did that!

65. What is the man's job?
66. How can the man be described?
67. How did the women feel about the man's behavior?

Questions 68 through 70 refer to the following conversation:
W: Do you think we ought to ask your boss to the dinner party? It might make up for all the time you had to have off sick last month.
M: I guess we could, but he can't be angry about the accident. There was nothing I could do about it, and it was their fault for having dangerous equipment in the factory.

W: Yes, but suing them didn't make you employee of the month, did it?
M: I doubt if you are gonna complain when the money comes through, though. That will pay for us to buy a nice new car. You've wanted one for months.
W: You have a point, but I just think you need to make an effort to get on well with everyone at work for a while until the whole thing is forgotten.

68. What happened to the man?
69. What did the man do?
70. What does the woman think the man should do?

Part 4

Directions: You will hear some talks given by a single speaker. You will be asked to answer three questions about what the speaker says in each talk. Select the best response to each question and mark the letter (A), (B), (C), or (D) on your answer sheet. The talks will not be printed in your test book and will be spoken only one time.

Questions 71 through 73 refer to the following news announcement:
And now for the economy. The latest round of flight cuts by major airlines could lead to higher fares. Airlines officials say excess capacity has pushed inflation-adjusted average fares to levels unseen since the late 1980s, resulting in billions of dollars in annual losses for the industry. With fewer seats to sell, airlines will try to reduce the number of seats that they sell at rock-bottom prices through internet discounters as they concentrate on bringing back higher-paying business travelers.

71. What might flight cuts result in?
72. In what year might airlines have experienced the same problem?
73. What will airlines now make an effort to do?

Questions 74 through 76 refer to the following announcement:
Your attention, please. There is a red Ford Taurus parked blocking the building's entryway. Will the owner of this vehicle please move it immediately? This area is meant for shuttle buses and taxis ONLY. You may move your car to either parking lot on the east or west side of the building. Again, this is a red Ford Taurus, license plate number 173 FTU. If it is still blocking the entrance 10 minutes from now, I am afraid we will have no choice but to call the towing company and have it removed. So please, will the owner of this red Ford Taurus move your vehicle immediately?

74. What kind of vehicle could be blocking the entryway?
75. Where is the Ford Taurus allowed to be parked?
76. What will happen if it is not moved in 10 minutes?

Questions 77 through 79 refer to the following commercial:
America loves to shop, and there's no place better than New Hampshire, where the shopping is sales tax-free and the choice is exceptional! Come browse through the interesting and unique shops from old-fashioned 5 cent and 10 cent stores to ski and sports shops featuring the latest equipment and fashions, nationally known names and brand factory outlets and one-of-a-kind boutiques. A bonus: many stores will ship your purchases so it's easy to say "yes" to that once-in-a-lifetime find. New Hampshire has a story to tell in the tradition of small home-based businesses and bustling workshops where craftspeople create items that reflect and contain the human spirit. For more on shopping, see listings by town within each region.

77. Besides variety, what else is heralded as being unique about shopping in New Hampshire?
78. What service do many stores provide?
79. What tradition does New Hampshire uphold?

Questions 80 through 82 refer to the following talk:
When you get a haircut at a hairdresser, or take your clothes to a dry-cleaner, or ask a garage to repair your car, you're buying a service. When you buy a service, you have the right to expect certain standards. First of all, the service must be completed within a reasonable time. This applies even if you and the person supplying the service have not agreed a time for the work to be finished by. Secondly, anyone who provides a service must do so with reasonable care and skill, to a proper standard of workmanship. If you paid someone to fix your roof because it was letting in water, it should not still leak after the work has been completed. Lastly, reliable and appropriate materials or goods should be used for the service. The same law covers goods and materials as if you were buying them directly.

80. Why are haircuts and car repairs mentioned?
81. When can reasonable timing of the service be expected?
82. Why is a leaky roof mentioned?

Questions 83 through 85 refer to the following talk:
Every time you breathe in, your lungs take in oxygen – the food for your brain and body cells. This is absorbed into your blood. Your heart pumps the blood around your body, where the cells take up the oxygen and get rid of the carbon dioxide and other waste products. The blood goes back via the heart to the lungs. In the lungs, blood gives up carbon dioxide (which you breathe out) and takes up more oxygen for the process to start again. Understanding how our body works can help us protect ourselves from heart attacks and strokes. Today, though, things are much better and heart attack and stroke victims can benefit from new medications and treatments unavailable to patients in years past.

83. What is considered as food for our brain?
84. When in the lungs, what does the blood give away?
85. What is the purpose of this text?

Questions 86 through 88 refer to the following talk:
Business names are no longer registered within any government departments. But there are laws about using certain names and disclosing certain details of ownership. Before 1982, many business names had to be registered under the Registration of Business Names Act 1916. The act was then repealed when new rules on business names came into force. This law was replaced by the Business Names Act 1985. This allows the Secretary of State to have certain controls over the name you choose for your business and what you must tell others about the ownership of the business. Some words and expressions are controlled by other laws. These rules protect the rights which persons may have in relation to names or words.

86. When was the Registration of Business Names Act repealed?
87. What does the Business Names Act allow?
88. What is the main purpose of the mentioned rules?

Questions 89 through 91 refer to the following talk:
The very first modern Olympic Games opened in the first week of April 1896. Pole-vaulting, sprints, shot put, weightlifting, swimming, cycling, target shooting, tennis, marathon, and gymnastics were all events at the first Olympics. The swimming events were held in the Bay of Zea in the Aegean Sea. Gold medalist Alfred Hoyos Guttmann described it: "I won ahead of the others with a big lead, but my greatest struggle was against the towering 12-foot waves and the terribly cold water." Approximately 300 athletes participated, representing 13 countries.

89. What is NOT a mentioned event at the first modern Olympics?
90. What was Alfred Hoyos Guttmann's biggest difficulty?
91. How many individuals participated in the first modern Games?

Questions 92 through 94 refer to the following announcement:
Our plane leaves at 7.30 tomorrow morning, so we will

leave the house at six o'clock sharp in order to get there an hour before departure time. I know it's early, so be sure to set your alarm so you don't oversleep. It is a nine-hour plane ride from New York to Greece. You have to remain seated during the trip, but there are many ways to entertain yourself. You could watch a movie, read a book, walk around, or take a nap. Once the plane lands in Greece, we will get our passports stamped. After that, we will get our luggage from the baggage claim and then catch a taxi and have it take us to Hotel Poseidon in Athens.

92. What time do they need to arrive at the airport?
93. Which is NOT a mentioned way they can entertain themselves on the plane?
94. Look at the graphic. Which one is their flight number?

Questions 95 through 97 refer to the following lecture:
All animals, but humans especially, adapt to their environments aided by learning. Through classical conditioning, we learn to anticipate events such as being fed or experiencing pain. Through operant conditioning, we learn to repeat acts that bring desired results and avoid acts that bring punishment. Through observational learning, we learn from the experience and example of others. Observational learning, where behaviors are observed and imitated, is a process found among higher animal groups such as humans. Modeling is the process of observing and imitating a specific behavior or action.

95. How do we learn how to prepare for events such as pain?
96. What do we learn to avoid through operant conditioning?
97. How are humans classified?

Questions 98 through 100 refer to the following talk:
Good morning, Mr Jones. This is Janet Fisher calling from Mr Samuels' office. Mr Samuels asked me to call you since he has to cancel today's meeting. I'm afraid he is not feeling well today. Mr Samuels has another meeting tomorrow at 10 and is flying to Dallas on Friday morning, not getting back until next Tuesday. Otherwise, he is available from 9 to 11 a.m. on weekdays. Let us know what suits you in order to reschedule. We are so sorry about the short notice.

98. What is Janet's job?
99. Look at the graphic. When is the rescheduled meeting likely to take place?
100. What does the woman mean when she says, "We are so sorry about the short notice."?

That is the end of the test.

TEST 3

In this section of the test, you will have the chance to show how well you understand spoken English. There are four parts to this section, with special directions for each part.

Part 1

Directions: For each question, you will see a picture and you will hear four short statements. The statements will be spoken just one time. They will not be printed in your test book so you must listen carefully to understand what the speaker says. When you hear the four statements, look at the picture and choose the statement that best describes what you see in the picture. Choose the best answer (A), (B), (C), or (D).
EXAMPLE:
Now listen to the four statements. You will hear:
(A) He is on the phone.
(B) She is driving the car.
(C) She is typing on the computer.
(D) He is sitting next to her.
Statement (D) best describes what you see in the picture. Therefore, you should choose answer (D).

1. (A) The men are acting.
(B) One man is taking a photograph.
(C) The man with the camera is pointing.
(D) The man with the headset is laughing.
2. (A) They are both wearing glasses.
(B) A man is receiving an award.
(C) A man is speaking into the microphone.
(D) They are in a board meeting.
3. (A) There is one woman in the front row.
(B) There are no empty seats.
(C) They are at the movie theater.
(D) A man is speaking.
4. (A) The patient is wearing a mask.
(B) The doctor is explaining something.
(C) The nurse is seated.
(D) The doctor is writing at his desk.
5. (A) They are boarding an airplane.
(B) The airplane is taking off.
(C) The airplane is grounded.
(D) They are inside an airplane.
6. (A) The two males are being interviewed.
(B) The boy is wearing a T-shirt.
(C) The man has one free hand.
(D) The girl is holding a cool drink.

Part 2

Directions: In this part of the test, you will hear a question or statement spoken in English, followed by three responses, also spoken in English. The question or statement and the responses will be spoken just one time. They will not be printed in your test book, so you must listen carefully. You are to choose the best response to each question or statement. Now listen to a sample question. You will hear:

Man: Why are you late?
Woman: (A) I hope I won't be.
(B) My car broke down.
(C) He always is.
The best response is choice B: "My car broke down". Therefore, you should choose B.

7. M: Have all the participants finished filling out the program evaluation?
W: A. Fifteen questions in total.
B. Just about.
C. No more than 20 minutes each.
8. W: You've just arrived from Honolulu, haven't you?
M: A. Yes. I leave tomorrow.
B. For about two weeks.
C. Yes, and I wish I could go back!
9. M: How can I get reimbursed for the supplies I bought for the presentation?
W: A. Submit your receipts to Kelsey Johnson.
B. I think it went extremely well.
C. Take a left and it's the first door on the right.
10. W: Can you recall what time the brunch is scheduled to begin?
M: A. It's a long and complicated schedule.
B. I believe it starts at 11.
C. They are serving eggs and pancakes.
11. M: Let's try that new restaurant Paul told us about.
W: A. OK. It sounds fantastic.
B. I'm a really good cook.
C. What is it about?
12. W: What time will she leave tomorrow?
M: A. At Gate 617.
B. By airplane.
C. Before lunchtime.
13. M: When will the renovations be completed?
W: A. It'll be a lot more modern.
B. By springtime.
C. It's going to cost the company a fortune.
14. W: Where did you buy the beautiful new couch?
M: A. From a catalog.
B. For the new house.
C. When I met her.
15. M: Could you tell me where the nearest bakery is?

W: A. I'm afraid it's closed this week.
B. There's one on the corner of Elm and Main.
C. Mostly pastries and cakes.

16. W: Is your manager's name Ron or Ross?
M: A. No, he's just the assistant manager.
B. I hope I get his position.
C. Neither. His name is Rod.

17. M: Have you sampled the cookies Joan made for the office yet?
W: A. No, but I heard they are to die for!
B. I don't want many, thank you.
C. I'll have it in by Monday.

18. W: You're aware of the fact that there's a large fee for late rent payment, aren't you?
M: A. Yes, don't worry. I always mail my check early.
B. No, because of rent control I pay a reasonable amount.
C. I never pay in cash.

19. M: Can I get you anything to drink while I am up?
W: A. No, I don't feel like going out.
B. An iced tea would be nice, if you don't mind.
C. I don't think you understood my question.

20. W: Are only people with graduate degrees being considered?
M: A. They get preference.
B. The commencement is scheduled for May 15.
C. Either one is acceptable.

21. M: Have you seen the latest poverty rates?
W: A. They're worth about one million dollars.
B. They're the highest they've been in decades.
C. Yes, I do.

22. W: How do I make a long-distance phone call?
M: A. Our associates in Spain are expecting a call.
B. Dial 9 to call outside the office, and then the country code and number.
C. It's about seven miles off the freeway exit.

23. M: What train is she taking?
W: A. I believe it's the 7.45.
B. As soon as she arrives.
C. The station is crowded today.

24. W: How long until the DSL connection is installed?
M: A. Sometime last year.
B. This is the conductor.
C. Before the month is up.

25. M: Did you manage to get an appointment for this week?
W: A. I tried, but she's completely booked.
B. No, I don't plan to.
C. My manager wanted to see you.

26. W: Jerry, do I have any new messages?
M: A. No, that's not what I mean.
B. Just Mr Tagland confirming your 2.30 conference call.
C. I will send that to Mr Falkey immediately.

27. M: Are they predicting sun for the weekend?
W: A. I hope so. I want to go to the beach.
B. No, he has a daughter.
C. Maybe, I haven't completely decided yet.

28. W: Would you like to carpool to the office?
M: A. It's too cold to go swimming.
B. There's no traffic that early in the morning.
C. Certainly. It makes sense since we live near each other.

29. M: Do you prefer reading the newspaper or learning about current events by watching the news on TV?
W: A. Reading is one of my favorite hobbies.
B. Nobody reads anymore because they are addicted to television.
C. By newspaper; that way I can select what I want to know.

30. W: Was Miami really hot in August?
M: A. Very much so; at least I had air-conditioning in my hotel.
B. I'll be back before the summer is over.
C. This place is full of retired citizens who have moved there to relax.

31. M: Do you recommend that I wait for the new model to come out?
W: A. No, stay inside where it is warm.
B. I think that would be the best idea.
C. Just a few more minutes.

Part 3

Directions: You will hear some conversations between two or more people. You will be asked to answer three questions about what the speakers say in each conversation. Select the best response to each question and mark the letter (A), (B), (C), or (D) on your answer sheet. The conversations will not be printed in your test book and will be spoken only one time.

Questions 32 through 34 refer to this conversation:
M: I'm gonna drive to the conference next week.
W: Why don't you fly?
M: The nearest airport is two hours from the center, so flying ultimately takes longer. Plus, I'd need a rental car.
W: Just be sure you record your mileage so you can be reimbursed. And watch out for bad weather!

32. Why doesn't the man fly to the conference?
33. How would the man have gotten from the airport to the conference center?
34. Why should the man keep track of his mileage?

Questions 35 through 37 refer to this conversation:
W: Our server, Gus, said that you wished to speak to me. I'm the manager.
M1: Yes. We waited 45 minutes for our food to arrive and all of our orders were incorrect.
M2: That's right, and we usually get good service here.
W: I am so sorry, and I will talk to Gus about this. Your meal will be on the house. And I will throw in some free cheesecakes.
M1: Thank you.

35. Where are they?
36. Why did the men want to speak to the manager?
37. What will the woman do after talking to the men?

Questions 38 through 40 refer to this conversation:
M1: Why should we hire you?
W: I have five years of experience doing the same job in Seattle. I am a committed employee and self-motivated.
M2: Now, this job would require you to work 60 hours a week. How do you feel about that?
W: That schedule is not for everyone, but I love dedicating myself wholly to something I love.

38. Who are the men in relationship to the woman?
39. Why did the man ask the woman why she should get the job?
40. How does the woman feel about working long hours?

Questions 41 through 43 refer to this conversation:
W: George? This is Moira. I won't be coming in today. I've got a fever.
M: Are there any meetings that I should cancel for you?
W: Just one. It's with Colleen about the new curriculum changes. Tell her I'll meet her as soon as I'm better.
M: And I'll tell everyone not to bother you on your cell.

41. Where is the woman?
42. What is going to happen with the curriculum change meeting?
43. What does the man promise to the woman?

Questions 44 through 46 refer to this conversation:
M: Is Tim enjoying the university?
W: He loves it. He's majoring in economics.
M: Wow, that is a lucrative field. Tony is a literature major. He loves it, but I worry that he won't make a good living. I think about discussing that with him, but my wife thinks we should let him decide his own path.
W: I agree with her 100 per cent.

44. Who are the man and woman?
45. What is the man worried about?
46. What does the woman think?

Questions 47 through 49 refer to this conversation:
M: How can I help you?
W: My computer just crashed. I'm looking for a laptop, but I am on a budget.
M: Will you be installing a lot of programs on the computer?
W: Oh no! I just use word processing.
M: Then let's take a look at these models over here.

47. Why does the woman want a new computer?
48. Look at the graphic. Which computer is the woman likely to get?
49. Why does the man ask the woman a question?

Questions 50 through 52 refer to this conversation:
M: I'm Tyler. I wanted to welcome you to East Publishing. How is your first day going?
W: It's a bit overwhelming, but it's not the worst first day I've ever had. Plus, everyone has been very friendly.
M: I'd be happy to treat you to lunch if you're interested. The cafeteria is surprisingly quite good. I love their lasagne!
W: Sounds great.

50. Why does the man stop by the woman's desk?
51. Why does the woman say, "It's a bit overwhelming."?
52. What is the man's opinion of the cafeteria food?

Questions 53 through 55 refer to this conversation:
M: We are out, but I can order it and have it in five days.
W: The birthday party is in two days.
M: We have other works by Dickens, like *Oliver Twist,* or other classic authors like Jane Austen.
W: I'm afraid she insists on *A Tale of Two Cities.*
M: Then I'd visit our Woodbury store. It's no short trip, but the only option.

53. Where are they?
54. What will the woman probably do?
55. Why does the man suggest another store?

Questions 56 through 58 refer to this conversation:
M: When we retire we can sleep in, take trips and finally have time to finish the house repairs.
W: Retirement? Thinking about it so soon is going to make the time drag on. Besides, you'll miss working.
M: I've been working since I was 16! I deserve some relaxation time.
W: Come on! You're always napping on the couch!

56. What is NOT a reason why the man wants to retire?
57. What is the woman's opinion on retiring?
58. What does the woman imply when she says, "You're always napping on the couch!"?

Questions 59 through 61 refer to this conversation:
W: I have a 3.30 appointment with Dr Nao. I know it's early, but I was in the neighborhood running errands. Can he see me now?
M: He is booked for the hour until your appointment. You can wait in the waiting room where there are magazines and a television.
W: That's OK. I'll just go read at the nearby coffee shop.

59. What time did the woman arrive at the doctor's office?
60. Why did the woman arrive at the office at the time she did?
61. What is the woman going to do while waiting for her appointment?

Questions 62 through 64 refer to this conversation:
W: Have you got everything that you need for the conference? You don't want a repeat of what happened last time when you went off without your laptop. Have you got your passport and your credit cards?

M: Yes, yes, stop fussing. Now, I will probably arrive late in the afternoon, but then we will be straight into a meeting so I won't be able to get in touch till last thing. So, don't worry if you don't hear from me till late.
W: I don't mind how late it is, dear, as long as you phone. Don't get too involved with all your friends and colleagues and forget.

62. What didn't the man have at the last conference?
63. When will the man phone?
64. What is the relationship between the speakers?

Questions 65 through 67 refer to this conversation:
M: What seems to be the problem?
W: I think my computer has crashed. It's completely dead and, since I only bought it two weeks ago, I'm very disappointed.
M: Let's see if I can talk you through it. It's always a bit difficult when you don't actually have the computer in front of you. Is there anything on the monitor at all?
W: No, I told you, it's dead. I've tried pressing all the buttons and clicking the mouse.
M: You don't have a power cut in your area, do you?
W: Oh, wait a minute. It's not plugged into the wall. Sorry.
M: It's an easy mistake to make, madam.

65. Where is the man?
66. What was the problem?
67. How does the man react?

Questions 68 through 70 refer to this conversation:
M: Hi, Susan, I'm afraid I'm a bit under the weather today, so I won't be coming in to the office.
W: OK, Ben, don't worry. The meeting has been canceled this morning anyway because too many people are on holiday. We'll sort out a day for next week to hold it.
M: Don't book it for Thursday as I'm going to the dentist in the morning.
W: OK, I'll try to finish your Jameson project if I get time.
M: Thanks Susan, I owe you one.

68. What is wrong with Ben?
69. What will happen about the meeting?
70. Why does the man say, "I owe you one."?

Part 4

Directions: You will hear some talks given by a single speaker. You will be asked to answer three questions about what the speaker says in each talk. Select the best response to each question and mark the letter (A), (B), (C), or (D) on your answer sheet. The talks will not be printed in your test book and will be spoken only one time.

Questions 71 through 73 refer to the following speech:
I was asked to speak to you future entrepreneurs about choosing a location for your business. I guess I would start out by suggesting that you find out if local zoning laws permit your kind of business at the site that you desire. It's also important to determine if there's adequate, affordable transportation. Can your employees get to work? Remember to consider the surrounding community. If you're a high-end retailer, for example, are there sufficient high-income households nearby to support your business? And lastly, look at the other businesses in the area. Decide whether or not having direct competitors will be helpful.

71 What do all the people listening to the speech have in common?
72. Look at the graphic. Which is likely to be the fourth point considered?
73. Why are high-income houses in the neighborhood important?

Questions 74 through 76 refer to the following forecast:
Good evening, Twin Cities. This is Paul Douglas with the national weather update. The forecast is shaping up and the southerners can expect a mild and calm week ahead. That is great news to many in Oklahoma, where thousands are still without power because of a crippling ice storm

that passed through over a week ago. It seems that if you want to find snow this winter, you actually have to head south instead of north. The storm brushed the Twin Cities; most of the Metro ended up with about a half inch to an inch of new snow. We can expect plenty of sunshine this afternoon. Your drive home from work could be slowed by a little light snow. This fast-moving clipper will be out of here by Wednesday morning, and the rest of the workweek is looking dry.

74. What happened in Oklahoma?
75. Where should you go if you want to see snow?
76. Look at the graphic. What can be concluded about the weather in Twin Cities?

Questions 77 through 79 refer to the following speech:
I appreciate your president having made me an honorary visiting professor, and I assure you that my first lecture will be very brief. I am delighted to be here, and I'm particularly delighted to be here on this occasion. The space effort has already created a great number of new companies and tens of thousands of new jobs. Space and related industries are generating new demands in investment and skilled personnel, and this city and this state and this region will share greatly in this growth. What was once the furthest outpost on the old frontier of the West will be the furthest outpost on the new frontier of science and space. Houston, your city of Houston, with its Manned Spacecraft Center, will become the heart of a large scientific and engineering community.

77. What does the speaker guarantee to the listeners?
78. What has their work already accomplished?
79. What will happen to Houston?

Questions 80 through 82 refer to the following talk:
This is such an exciting meal that can be made in no time. And the best part about it is that it is just as delicious as it is healthy. OK, first of all, in a big bowl, combine cherry tomatoes, green olives, black olives, and spring onions. Then, in a dry skillet, toast pine nuts over medium heat until golden brown, turning frequently. Then, stir them into the tomato mixture. Next, in a small bowl, mix together olive oil, red wine vinegar, sugar, and oregano. Season to taste with salt and pepper. And lastly, pour the sauce over the vegetables and gently stir so it coats.

80. What is NOT true of the meal being prepared?
81. What needs to be put over heat?
82. What is being prepared?

Questions 83 through 85 refer to the following speech:
These points are simple but extremely important. Remember to speak with conviction as if you really believe in what you are saying. Persuade your audience effectively. The material you present orally should have the same ingredients as that required for a written research paper: for example, have an introduction, body, and conclusion. Do not read from notes for any extended length of time, although it is quite acceptable to glance at your notes infrequently. Speak loudly and clearly. Sound confident. Do not mumble. If you make an error, correct it and continue. No need to make excuses or apologize profusely.

83. What is the point of the speech?
84. What should speakers do with their notes?
85. What should speakers do if they make a mistake?

Questions 86 through 88 refer to the following advertisement:
Are you someone who wants to get a quality education without having to commit your entire life to obtaining it? Perhaps you need to work. Perhaps you have a family. Perhaps you learn better in a freer environment. Perhaps you need to study at your own pace. If these things are true, then American Community College is for you. We specifically only offer weekday evening classes, weekend classes, or even classes via the internet from the comfort of your home. Call or email to enroll and start your journey to a successful life!

86. Why does the speaker say, "Perhaps you need to work."?
87. What type of class could you NOT take through the school?
88. What part of the school does the advertisement focus on?

Questions 89 through 91 refer to the following announcement:
Thank you for your patience. The mechanical problem has now been taken care of. We will now start preboarding for Flight 717 to Tampa, Florida. If you need extra assistance boarding the plane or have a child or infant, you may now begin the boarding process. Momentarily we will begin boarding those passengers seated in the first-class section, and then we will board alphabetically by zones. Please locate your zone on your ticket. We have a full flight today, so please be sure to only board when your zone is called. Lastly, would passengers Engel and Drews please approach the ticket counter? Thank you.

89. Why does the speaker say, "Thank you for your patience."?
90. What is NOT true of the plane?
91. Why must passengers only board when called to do so?

Questions 92 through 94 refer to the following talk:
Excuse me, sir. I've noticed that you are just leaving the State Fair. I'm Shelly O'Brien with Channel 8 and was hoping you would have a few minutes to tell our viewers at home about your time at the fair. We, along with the entire tri-state, are very interested in learning what people's highlights were. For example, what rides and musical entertainment did you enjoy most? And we are of course most interested in knowing what the tastiest thing you ate was! So could you please share some of your thoughts with us before you head for your car?

92. Where is this encounter taking place?
93. What does Shelly work for?
94. What highlight is Shelly especially interested in?

Questions 95 through 97 refer to the following speech:
Good morning, everyone, and I hope you all enjoyed your breakfast – I know I did. As always, I just have a few general announcements before the sessions begin at nine. As you all know, today is our last day, which of course means that we need to end with a little bit of fun. The meetings will end an hour earlier than usual. So we will be done at 5.30, today. Then dinner will be served at the dining hall in the Radcliffe Building, not here in Stowe Hall where we usually eat. Our final party will be in the Olmstead Room, right next to the dining hall, and will commence immediately following the meal. Finally, the shuttle buses will be in the parking lot awaiting us at eight sharp tomorrow morning to take us to the airport.

95. Where is this announcement taking place?
96. When do the meetings normally conclude?
97. Look at the graphic. Which of the following would best describe the event?

Questions 98 through 100 refer to the following talk:
Good evening and welcome to tonight's performance of *Romeo and Juliet*. We do ask that you not take any flash photography during the performance and that no recording devices of any kind are used. And please turn off all cellular telephones, beepers, or any other devices that may interrupt the performance. At the end of Act 1, there will be a 20-minute intermission where you are free to leave your seats. There will be refreshments served in the lobby, and the bathrooms are located to the right of the entrance and down the hall. Unless there is an emergency, please wait until intermission before leaving the auditorium. After the performance, the actors will be in the lobby for autographs and pictures. Thank you, and again, enjoy the performance.

98. What is NOT something the audience should refrain from?
99. What does the speaker give directions for?
100. What will the actors be doing after the performance?

That is the end of the test.

TEST 1

Listening – Part 1: Photographs

1. (C) In this picture, we can see that the woman's body is indicative of a woman expecting a child.
(A) The picture shows that the woman is still pregnant and has not given birth yet.
(B) The picture shows that another woman is touching her stomach; she isn't touching her own.
(D) The picture clearly shows that the woman's dress has no sleeves, as her arms are showing.

2. (C) This picture shows people sitting around a dining room table and sitting on toilets, which are strange seats to be sitting on while at a table.
(A) There is only one candle centered on the table, not more than one.
(B) The picture shows that the people have not been given any food yet and there are no waiters/waitresses serving food either.
(D) The picture does not appear to show the people in a bathroom, the room is large and there is no other bathroom furniture. It is just that the people are sitting on toilets, which are usually found in bathrooms.

3. (A) The picture shows two women who have their babies in their strollers and are walking down the street.
(B) The babies are not being carried, which would suggest that the women were holding the babies. The babies are inside their strollers.
(C) The women are not on the sidewalk but instead on the crossing, crossing the street.
(D) They are not on a busy street, as the picture shows only a few cars; some are parked and only one is moving.

4. (D) The picture shows a woman gesturing as if she is speaking; her facial expressions appear as if she is speaking. The man is still; he is facing the woman and is paying attention to her.
(A) In the picture, the man is sitting still and his arms aren't raised.
(B) In the picture, there doesn't appear to be anything on the woman's legs, i.e., her lap.
(C) The man and woman are sitting opposite one another, not next to each other.

5. (C) In the picture, the woman is dressed in a smart red dress, and her surroundings suggest that her dress is formal.
(A) The picture shows the man wearing a suit with a bow tie, so he is not wearing casual clothes.
(B) The picture shows the man holding the microphone, not the woman.
(D) The woman isn't talking directly to the man; rather, he has spoken to her. She is not looking towards him, but away.

6. (A) The stepladder, which is a small ladder used to reach high places, is standing separately from the men. No one is standing on the stepladder.
(B) The picture shows two men; one is standing and the other is kneeling down; they are not both kneeling on the floor.
(C) The picture shows that the men are holding hammers and using these to put nails in the wall. It doesn't show that the men have cloths to polish.
(D) There doesn't appear to be a hammer on the ground; rather, the two men are both holding hammers.

Listening – Part 2: Question–Response

7. (B) As the question asks about the time, it is looking for a specific number (time). The answer doesn't ask for a date and it doesn't refer to the future, so it cannot be (A). (C) Is incorrect because the question isn't asking for your opinion on whether they will be on time or not.

8. (C) The question asks 'where' so requires a response giving a place. It does not ask 'when' so doesn't require a time like in (A). Choice (B) answers the question, 'Who are you going with?'

9. (C) The man wants to know who the person living in the house is, so the correct reply would be a specific person. (A) is incorrect because the question doesn't ask if the woman herself lives in the house. Choice (B) is a reply to a question asking how big the house is or how many bedrooms it has.

10. (A) This question suggests that there is a problem with the phone, so the man agrees it is not working. (B) doesn't show that the phone is having problems; there can't be a message since there is a problem. (C) is incorrect, because the question doesn't ask the woman to phone the man.

11. (C) The question asks whether the woman liked the film and the answer confirms she did. Choice (A) is formed in the future tense, but the question is formed in the past, suggesting that they have already seen the film. (B) is incorrect as the answer is formed as if it is a regular occurrence.

12. (B) This answer gives a particular name, as the question is asking what the cafe is called. (A) confirms a name and assumes the man already knows the name. (C) says the cafe isn't far. The question does not ask for the distance to the cafe.

13. (C) The question asks 'when', so the answer requires a particular date and for an answer that is in the future. (A) is a question; the answer requires a statement – some information. (B) The woman doesn't need to give him a present.

14. (C) The question is asking for someone to help with the letter writing. The man says that he will be able to do it for the woman. (A) The man does not require a stamp to send his letter. (B) The man offers some paper, but again the woman does not request anything to write the letter with.

15. (A) The question asks if the meeting is still in the same place; the woman omits answering yes or no but assumes yes because of what the memo said. (B) gives the time, although the question doesn't ask when it is. (C) gives directions, but the question doesn't ask for a specific location.

16. (C) The question is inquiring whether the man works for Mrs Brown. The man's answer corrects the woman and says he actually works for Mr Davies. (A) The woman isn't asking if the man needs help. (B) is an answer to the question 'Can you help me?', but the woman doesn't require assistance herself.

17. (B) The woman uses the word 'Certainly' to emphasize what she is saying when she makes a statement; she replies 'yes' positively. (A) The question is asking for the future, but this answer is formed in the past. The woman denies taking the photo, but the man asks if she could take the photo. (C) uses the word 'picture' in the sense of drawing, but the question uses 'picture' meaning 'photograph'.

18. (C) The question is asking for the man's preference to the food; the man's response is that he likes both. (A) The question doesn't ask for the whereabouts of the food. (B) gives a choice of food, but the question doesn't ask whether he would like beer.
19. (C) The question asks about a reason. The woman is guessing it could be because he didn't get on the bus. (A) doesn't say the reason why he is late, just that he is regularly late. (B) is also incorrect, as the question does not ask for the amount of time he is late by.
20. (A) The woman wants to know whether the man is ready to say what he would like. The man replies he isn't ready yet and would like more time. (B) suggests that the man is taking the order, but it is the other way round. (C) is praise for a selection from an order, but it is the man who is supposed to be ordering.
21. (C) The man is inquiring if he has received anything; the message could be by post or telephone. The woman replies that she does have a message for him. (A) is incorrect because it is as if the man is asking the woman if she has spoken. (B) is incorrect, as the man is asking if he has any messages; he would not know himself what the message would be if he had one.
22. (A) The woman inquires whether the man would like to play tennis with her. The man is very happy to and agrees to play with her. (B) uses the word 'join' in the wrong way: it uses 'join' to mean 'become a member of something'. The 'join' in the question asks if they would like to take part. (C) is incorrect because they have not played the game yet, so the man could not have an opinion on whether the tennis match was good or not.
23. (B) The question inquires about the length of time. The woman tells the man how long she has been there – since she was young. (A) is incorrect, as the question does not ask how long the woman has been looking for a house. (C) answers as if the man has brought her a present for moving into her house.
24. (A) The woman is questioning whether the briefcase belongs to Ben. The man agrees and says he is certain it does. (B) uses the word 'brief' in an incorrect way; the brief here means 'short'. The brief in the question refers to a case used to carry documents. (C) is incorrect; the man is asking a question. He does not make a statement that the briefcase is Ben's.
25. (C) The man is inquiring about whether the coat is on discount. The woman replies that it is and it is half the usual price. (A) The question is asking whether the coat is on sale, so the answer can't be about having a blue coat. (B) uses the word 'sale' to mean 'sail' as used in a boat on water. The question doesn't refer to sailing and the woman's preference for it.
26. (C) The woman wants to know a name. The man replies with what the new secretary is called. (A) The question doesn't ask where the secretary is. (B) The question doesn't ask how good the new secretary is at her work.
27. (B) The question wants to know whether the food has been made yet. The woman replies it has been made and it is waiting on the table. (A) The question isn't asking whether the woman is prepared herself. (C) The word 'prepared' in this question refers to preparing a meal – mixing food together – not that something has broken and needs to be repaired.
28. (C) The question is asking whether someone would like to go to the theater. The man replies in agreement that he likes the woman's idea. (A) The word 'treat' in this question means something special has been arranged for enjoyment, not that a doctor or nurse treats a patient for an illness. (B) The question is not referring to treatment by a doctor or about a hospital. This answer suggests the theater is next to the hospital.
29. (B) The man inquires whether the work that the woman has been doing is completed yet. The woman replies that she hasn't finished it yet, but is near to finishing. (A) This answer refers to the word 'report', meaning a broadcast from the news, but the question is referring to a piece of work. (C) The question is not referring to a journalist or a reporter of news. It is not asking about the quality of work.
30. (B) The woman wants to know if the man wants food. The man replies that he does and he is extremely hungry. (A) This question is not asking if the man is 'angry', but instead 'hungry', so the man's reply does not refer to food. (C) The question does not ask whether the man has time to eat or not.
31. (C) The man is asking the woman whether she is unwell, whether she has a cold. The woman replies that she has been unwell and has had a cold for a while. (A) The man is not asking if the woman feels cold in temperature, but if she has a cold, an illness. (B) is incorrect, as the man is referring to the woman and does not ask about someone else.

Listening – Part 3: Conversations
32. (B) Megan is unsure because she does not know if her presentation is at the right level for her audience.
33. (C) Megan is planning ahead; she doesn't have to give her presentation until the 10th and she has already finished it.
34. (A) Michael says he has a packed schedule but has free time on the 5th and will help Megan.
35. (C) She wants to do voluntary work with disabled children.
36. (B) The woman needs to come back the next morning. Anna, the person who deals with volunteers, doesn't work in the afternoon.
37. (A) The man is very helpful; he provides information and solutions for the woman.
38. (D) The woman is annoyed because she will not be able to make the flight that was booked.
39. (B) The man made the mistake because he did not get the required information from Elsie.
40. (C) The woman is not available on Thursday because she has to work until 8 p.m.
41. (B) The woman would like to be at the seaside with her kids and Todd.
42. (C) The man jokingly suggests that they should be allowed to take 'sun days' like sick days.
43. (B) They are coworkers as they are sitting behind computers and also talk about their manager.
44. (D) The woman says she knows others are having problems too and she'll try to arrange an extension.
45. (A) The man wanted to inform the woman that he won't finish his report on time.
46. (D) The man refers to Ms Johnson in a polite way, and she deals with the situation with authority.

47. (B) Her eyes were sparkling and she had a huge smile when she told the woman the news about the job offer.
48. (C) The woman answers that she thinks Laura might take the job because she looked happy.
49. (B) The man says that Australia is far away and she would miss her family.
50. (C) The man was surprised because he thought the woman had been excited about it last week.
51. (B) The woman feels she would probably only use it at weekends.
52. (C) He thinks if she rented a car she would be much less likely to go on a trip
53. (C) She doesn't know what to do and feels uncomfortable about why her workmate doesn't speak to her.
54. (C) She's unhappy because unless she speaks first, her workmate acts as if she doesn't see her.
55. (A) He tells the woman to ask her workmate if it bothers her if she talks to her.
56. (D) The man really can't stand tomatoes.
57. (B) The man says it's not the end of the world if he doesn't eat the salad because he has the steak and chips as well.
58. (D) The woman apologizes and offers to bring the man another salad.
59. (A) The woman tells him his design for the park was original and fun.
60. (A) The man really enjoyed it and said it was a fun space to work with.
61. (B) The woman is pleased they got the contract and thanks him for his hard work.
62. (A) A couple was interested in buying a house in town this week; therefore, that would be Mr and Mrs Phillips, according to the graphic.
63. (C) He doesn't know what to do with himself all day.
64. (D) She will go to the store for a bite to eat.
65. (C) They are discussing the memo for the design meeting, not the meeting about the Parson Project.
66. (B) She thinks management will be their usual annoying selves.
67. (B) He is tired of the meetings and would prefer to get on with the job.
68. (A) The man thought it was her dream house, so he was surprised when he was told she wasn't going to get it.
69. (A) They are referring to an over-budget house, with the budget being 200,000; therefore, that is the countryside house, according to the graphic.
70. (D) He says she should rethink what is really important to her.

Listening – Part 4: Talks

71. (C) The building is a gallery of the Bradford family's art collection.
72. (D) The Bradford family made their fortune from making and selling beautiful clothes.
73. (A) Charles Bradford is the great-grandfather of Alan Bradford.
74. (C) This change of platform is due to a problem with the signals.
75. (A) The express train to Atlanta is now departing at 11.30; therefore, it is the 58963 train, according to the graphic.
76. (D) As there have been signal problems, the Washington train leaves from platform four.
77. (C) John will be serving them tonight, so he's a waiter.
78. (A) Today's delicious specials are grilled salmon, roast chicken, mixed grill, and steak with pepper.
79. (C) He says that he will bring the dessert trolley round later, as there are too many tasty things to mention.
80. (B) The programme is called 'The Sky at Night'; they have a special guest to talk about light pollution.
81. (A) The amount of light pouring into the night sky has increased by a quarter in the past 10 years – 25%.
82. (C) Next they will speak to an expert, but first they play some music.
83. (C) This week there will be a series of 12 films about human relationships.
84. (D) The film is characterized as moving, therefore easily making someone feel sad or down, that is, breaking their heart.
85. (A) After the film, the guests are invited to a cheese and wine reception.
86. (C) The announcement is targeted at shoppers to inform them about that day's bargains and special offers.
87. (B) On the top floor, The Coffee Place has a special offer of a free cake with each drink purchased.
88. (C) The late night shopping finishes at 8 p.m., which is only four hours away. So the time now is 4 p.m.
89. (A) They are aboard the Skybird International Flight 362 from London to Cape Town, waiting to depart.
90. (B) The announcement is being made on behalf of the captain and the rest of the cabin crew by a cabin crew member.
91. (C) The journey from London to Paris is expected to last 1 hour and 10 minutes; therefore, because of the time difference, they should leave London at 7.00 (GMT) if they are to arrive in Paris at 9.10 (GMT +1 hour), according to the graphic.
92. (A) There is a problem with the computer and it needs to be fixed.
93. (D) The man says he will try to fix the computer over the phone.
94. (C) The first thing the man asks is if the computer is connected to the internet.
95. (B) A radio announcer is speaking, saying, 'Good morning, this is the 9 o'clock business news!'
96. (A) Investment banks have already predicted that the US economy will fall into recession in two years' time.
97. (A) Consumer spending accounts for two-thirds of the US economy.
98. (B) The announcer says he wants to extend a warm welcome to the delegates.
99. (D) The conference has taken place twice before, as this is the third annual event.
100. (C) The announcer informs everyone that the presentations begin promptly at 9 a.m. the following morning.

Reading – Part 5: Incomplete Sentences

101 D. Although John found his manager hard to get along with, he did the best he could.
After 'although', we use a subject and a verb. It also shows contrast. We could say: 'John found his manager

hard to get along with. Nevertheless, he did the best he could.' If we start a sentence with 'so', we use inversion.
102 C. He was forced to declare bankruptcy two years after purchasing the property for his business because he couldn't make the payments. The word 'bankruptcy' is the correct answer, because he couldn't make the payments. Bankruptcy = when you are declared in law as being unable to pay your debts.
103 B. Although his new job had long hours, Mike was pleased with his higher salary. Salary is the money you earn every month or every year from your job.
104 C. Be sure to submit your application form by the 20th of March if you wish to be considered for the post. The first conditional with 'if' here shows that this is possible to happen in the present or future.
105 D. I am finishing the report now; I'll be with you in a second. The present continuous is used here to say what is in progress now.
106 D. The day of the meeting has been changed; it has been rescheduled for Thursday. Scheduled = to arrange something for a different time. 'Rectify' means to correct something.
107 A. On one hand, we've had a bit of a setback, but on the other hand, it's a chance to show that we're determined to make this business flourish again. We use 'on one hand ... on the other hand' to show contrast.
108 A. Be sure to let me know if I can be of any assistance. If we say 'Can I be of any assistance?' we mean 'Can I help you?'
109 D. Due to a lapse in security, hackers got access to the company's files. Lapse (in something) = a mistake that is made because of a temporary lack of attention to something.
110 C. Lunch will be served after the meeting, when you will have a chance to have an informal chat with the new boss. We need future passive here to talk about something that will happen.
111 D. Although one of the two candidates has more experience, the other has great enthusiasm and energy. We can use 'the other' to refer to a second person or thing, so we say, 'one of the two candidates ... the other'.
112 A. The bus is departing promptly so please hurry up, otherwise you will be late for work. 'Promptly' is an adverb and we can use adverbs to add more information about the verb.
113 B. Does the position include any benefits, such as a company car or health insurance? Benefit = a payment made by the state or an insurance scheme to somebody who is entitled to it. We can say 'productivity/performance bonuses', but we say 'unemployment benefit', 'child benefit', etc.
114 C. Many were worried the country would suffer a recession because of the rise in interest rates. Recession = a period when the economy of a country is not doing well.
115 B. The folder in which you will find the report is on the top shelf. In which = where. We can also replace 'in which' with 'where'.
116 B. It is important that you raise any concerns you might have so we can address them. The collocation 'raise concerns' means saying that you are worried about something.
117 A. She doesn't like wearing a uniform at work. She is the kind of person who likes to dress to impress. Infinitive is required here. 'Dress to impress' is also a phrase.
118 B. Michelle felt like she was kept on the sidelines and was not really considered part of the team. If somebody is watching something from the sidelines, or is kept on the sidelines, they are observing a situation rather than being directly involved in it.
119 D. Amy decided to specialize in cardiology after graduating from medical school. People can specialize in a particular field, such as cardiology, physiotherapy, etc.
120 A. The hierarchy within the company was very complex. 'Within' or 'in' could be correct here.
121 C. Anna was concerned about keeping her job because the company was downsizing. When we use the word 'downsize' to refer to a company, it means that the company is reducing the number of staff.
122 B. Profits were marginal; better than last year, but still short of our goal. When the word 'marginal' is used in economics, it means producing just enough income to cover the costs of making and selling something.
123 A. I'm afraid I'm exhausted; I've been working in the office since 7 a.m. 'Exhausted' means 'very tired', and it is the only word that makes sense here. 'Invigorate' means to make someone feel energetic and fresh, and 'incensed' means very angry.
124 A. Mario felt that he did not get enough recognition for his hard work. If you get recognition for your work, it means that people at work will say or show to you that you have done a good job.
125 D. Alison, like her sister Jessica, is studying to be a lawyer. The clause 'like her sister Jessica' is used between commas to add information to the sentence 'Alison is studying to be a lawyer'.
126 B. I would like to thank you for your cooperation in reaching a speedy solution to the unexpected problems of the merging of the two businesses. We say 'your cooperation in doing something'.
127 A. Ann is going to attend an interview for the position of Assistant Director on Thursday. The form 'be going to' is used to show what Ann intends to do in the near future.
128 B. Although you were working under pressure, you have done an excellent job! 'Although' shows contrast, and after 'although' we use a subject and a verb.
129 D. The check bounced because the account was empty and he was charged a fee. We use the word 'bounce' when we talk about a check. Bounce = to cause a check to not be paid or accepted by a bank because of lack of money in the account.
130 B. In order to be efficient, you must focus on the task at hand. We say 'focus on' or 'concentrate on'.

Reading – Part 6: Text Completion
131 B. ... we're <u>raising</u> money for the children's' charity *Future Horizons* to buy computers ... . When we talk about charity, we 'raise money'. We usually raise money to help people in need.
132 A. ... Bring your family and friends; everyone is welcome. <u>Please get tickets from me or from Sophia Johnson.</u> They invite all employees and their families so children are allowed. They also

encourage everybody to go to the barbecue, so it is not mandatory.

133 A. I hope to see you there! We also say 'I hope I will see you'; the gerund 'seeing' is not possible.

134 C. PS. In case of bad weather, there will be a marquee erected in the park. In case of bad weather = If the weather is bad. Option B shows contrast that doesn't make sense.

135 D. Tuberculosis is a bacterial disease which causes infection, most commonly in the lungs, but occasionally in other body organs. It says it causes infection mainly in the lungs, and then it uses the word 'but' to refer to other organs, so we understand that other organs can be affected fewer times.

136 B. 48 to 72 hours after the injection, the forearm is examined. For most individuals, a swelling that measures 10 mm or more indicates that the person has been in contact with tuberculosis. Words that make sense here are 'shows', 'indicates,' etc.

137 A. Mantoux tests may be required for new employees, volunteers, residents, and clients of some organizations and institutions. 'May' is a modal verb, so it is followed by an infinitive without 'to'. Options A and B have the infinitive 'be', but option B is active. Option A is correct, because it means that Mantoux may be needed for new employees (passive).

138 B. All people who have come in contact with a person with active tuberculosis should be tested as soon as possible, and again, three months after the date of last contact. 'Come in contact with' is a phrase that means 'touch or come very near'.

139 D. I would like to recommend that you consider applying, … In this context, 'consider' means to spend time thinking about the possibility (of applying). The person who writes the letter recommends that Mr Jones should apply for the position.

140 D. … since the work that you have already done for our company on a freelance basis makes you highly qualified for the position. The employee is qualified for this position (qualified = having the skills, experience, or training needed).

141 C. The job offers flexible working hours, as well as comprehensive health benefits. The correct answer is 'as well as' because it means 'in addition to'. 'As such' means 'in the exact sense of the word.'

142 D. If you have any questions, or would like more information, please feel free to contact me by email, or at 247 775 5674 ext: 239. The phrase 'feel free (to do something)' means 'have no hesitation or shyness (about doing something).'

143 D. I am on the job hunt for another team member. Option C cannot be correct because of the word 'unpaid'; the advertisement says 'Salary to be discussed'. Options A & B do not talk about the new role at all.

144 B. This person will be based in our Auckland, NZ, office, will manage a range of email marketing, and will lead generation campaigns for our growing list of clients. An employee can be 'based' in an office. They cannot be 'homed', and in this case, they cannot be 'replaced' as they are asking for an employee; they are not replacing one. We use the word 'found' if we are looking for somebody.

145 B. This role will suit those who have a few years' work experience in web development with some client-facing involvement and can show an ability and desire to uncover all there is to know about online marketing. 'Those' refers to the people that are described in this sentence. We can also say, 'This role will suit those people who have …'.

146 C. If you are interested in knowing more, then it is probably best to use the sales inquiry form to kick things off. We use the noun 'inquiry', because this is an 'inquiry form'. Using the noun is the usual way of describing a form. Another example is 'an application form'.

Reading – Part 7: Reading Comprehension

Questions 147–148

147. The correct answer is (C); The card gives information about what to do if oxygen levels become low during a flight.

148. The correct answer is (D); the mask will be released from above your head and the card says to pull the mask gently towards you.

Questions 149–151

149. The correct answer is (A); to ensure a table at SkyCity, a reservation is recommended.

150. The correct answer is (C); the advertisement says that between May 31st and September 3, groups of 10 or more cannot be accommodated. So May 3rd would be allowed with a reservation.

151. The correct answer is (A); according to the text, reservations on a Friday for lunch are 11.00 a.m.–3.00 p.m. and for dinner 5.00 p.m.–10.00 p.m.

Questions 152–154

152. The correct answer is (A); the leaflet speaks about their Michelin-trained chef and also says that when you go to the Sydney Opera House, you are welcomed with a glass of sparkling wine. These features are presented to entice the customer.

153. The correct answer is (A); high teas, exquisite food, sparkling wine, and a performance by an opera singer are all included.

154. The correct answer is (D); the text says 'Bookings are essential'.

Questions 155–157

155. The correct answer is (B); the email says that 'I'm sending this out to remind everyone that …'.

156. The correct answer is (D); the sessions run in the morning and afternoon. Employees can sign up for their preference.

157. The correct answer is (B); the email says that both sessions should take about four hours each, one in the morning and one in the afternoon.

Questions 158–160

158. The correct answer is (D); it is advised that you close the door to confine the smoke and fire.

159. The correct answer is (D); when you phone 911, it is advised that you identify yourself and tell the dispatcher the exact location of the fire or smoke and what is burning.

160. The correct answer is (D); 'This' refers to the personnel assembling in a specific location, as mentioned in the previous sentence.

Questions 161–163

161. The correct answer is (C); it's notifying a travel insurance company that luggage has been lost and informing them of the cost of replacing it.

162. The correct answer is (C); the policy is valid up until August 1st.

163. The correct answer is (B); the lost luggage included clothing, and camping and climbing equipment.

Questions 164–166

164. The correct answer is (C); the duration for train V344 is five hours and 25 minutes.

165. The correct answer is (C); the V344 train arrives in Michigan City at 13.39, while the others all arrive after 14.00.

166. The correct answer is (B); you have to change three times. The other trains have only two changes.

Questions 167–169

167. The correct answer is (B); it's presented by 'Filmhouse' and is an exhibition of photos and film.

168. The correct answer is (A); the exhibition is showing on Wednesday 17th October from 2–4.30 p.m.

169. The correct answer is (D); it showcases how young people have explored what remains important to them about their own heritage.

Questions 170–172

170. The correct answer is (C); the cost is £5 per person, not including entry to the gardens.

171. The correct answer is (B); according to the leaflet prebooking is essential.

172. The correct answer is (A); the phrase is followed by the assumption that it was raining during their visit, which shows that this is something to be expected.

Questions 173–175

173. The correct answer is (C); notice of holiday must now be given no less than one month before the intended date. In the past, it used to be just one week.

174. The correct answer is (B); it will enable them to employ temporary help if necessary.

175. The correct answer is (C); there is a form you must fill out to provide notice.

Questions 176–180

176. The correct answer is (B); the text advertises the conference hall and speaks about the size and how many delegates it can hold. It also says they work closely with the clients to make the perfect venue.

177. The correct answer is (B); the letter is in reply to Ms Fisher's inquiry about their company.

178. The correct answer is (B); in the letter, Bob is delighted to hear Ms Fisher has chosen the city of Victoria to host her conference.

179. The correct answer is (A); the leaflet says that the conference center is located in the heart of downtown Victoria, British Columbia.

180. The correct answer is (A); the address at the top of the page confirms that Ms Fisher is from Bristol in the UK.

Questions 181–185

181. The correct answer is (C); the letter warns people they will be without electricity for a period of time.

182. The correct answer is (C); the letter says there will be no power for approximately four hours on the morning of September 12th.

183. The correct answer is (D); the insert advises that candles should not be left unattended.

184. The correct answer is (B); the insert advises people to turn off sensitive electronic appliances such as computers.

185. The correct answer is (B); the insert suggests not to open fridges more than necessary, but doesn't mention anything about defrosting them.

Questions 186–190

186. The correct answer is (A); in the email, Tara says she went to the restaurant yesterday.

187. The correct answer is (D); Tara says the food was really something.

188. The correct answer is (B); Tara describes the restaurant as having 'a rather elegant clientele'.

189. The correct answer is (C); lunch is served from Tuesday to Saturday from midday (that is, 12 p.m. to 3 p.m.).

190. The correct answer is (B); according to the job vacancy, 'vegetarian and vegan cuisine' is their 'speciality'.

Questions 191–195

191. The correct answer is (B); the notice advertises the 'Online Banking Course', and you can learn how to use online banking to your advantage.

192. The correct answer is (A); the letter is a reply to Mr Woodhouse and gives information about the number of places and options available.

193. The correct answer is (C); the evening courses run on Tuesday and Thursday evenings from 7–9 p.m.

194. The correct answer is (D); the weekend courses run for two weekends on Saturday and Sunday, lasting for four days in total.

195. The correct answer is (D); they will no longer find online banking tricky if they attend the course.

Questions 196–197

196. The correct answer is (B); the email thanks Mr Rogers for his enquiry.

197. The correct answer is (D); the previous section mentions the Wired for Business Plan for the first time, so the sentence referring to the leaflet about this plan will follow.

Questions 198–200

198. The correct answer is (B); wireless internet access is available in all public spaces in the hotel.

199. The correct answer is (B); he is texting his business partner who has been to the hotel before to ask him for more information.

200. The correct answer is (D); the plan includes only local phone calls and unlimited long distance-calls within the US.

TEST 2

Listening – Part 1: Photographs

1. (C) In this picture, we can see the speaker (a woman) is standing behind the podium, a platform on which she is standing to speak to the audience.
(A) They are not applauding or clapping the speaker; the other people are standing still with their arms in front of them. (B) We are unable to see the speaker's arms, so we don't know if she is moving them or not. (D) One lady on the left is looking down, but everyone else is looking towards the speaker.

2. (D) The picture shows that the people are outside and going onto the plane to board. (A) The plane is not taking

off, as it has not left the ground. (B) The passengers are not seated, as they are still standing and haven't fully entered the plane yet. (C) The passengers are not disembarking, as they are not leaving the plane after a journey. They are queuing towards the plane to get on.
3. (B) The woman on the far left, wearing glasses, is speaking, because her arm is raised gesturing and her mouth is slightly open.
(A) In the picture, we can only see one man wearing a tie. (C) Two of the women are crossing their legs; the woman on the far left has her legs uncrossed. (D) The picture shows that only one woman is speaking; the other people are sitting still and are focusing on the woman on the far left.
4. (A) The picture shows the papers are scattered on the table; they are spread out over it in an untidy and irregular way. (B) The men in the picture appear to be seated next to one another at the corner of the table. (C) Two men are looking at one document; the man on the left is looking at his own piece of paper. (D) Notebooks, being small books in which to write, are not present on the table.
5. (B) The picture shows that the man has a narrow piece of material, a strap, on his right shoulder.
(A) The man is not saluting the flag – addressing it in a formal fashion; he has his arm low by his side as if gesturing while talking.
(C) The woman doesn't look like she is unhappy with the man; rather, she has a smile on her face.
(D) The woman isn't avoiding looking at the man straight in his face; her head is raised and she is looking straight at him.
6. (A) The picture shows that the man second from the left is wearing jeans – casual blue trousers. (B) The woman in the picture is holding her book. (C) The man on the far left wearing a sleeveless jacket has not got a beard. His lower face has no hair. (D) All the people in the picture, including the woman, are wearing name tags – a small cord worn around the neck with a badge showing someone's name on it.

Listening – Part 2: Question–Response
7. (C) The question asks about a time, so the woman answers saying the time when her plane will leave. (A) suggests the plane has already left. (B) doesn't give a time but only a hope that her plane will leave. The question assumes the plane will definitely leave.
8. (B) The woman is asking for a preference; the man replies saying what type of movie he likes. (A) The question doesn't ask where you get the movies from that you watch. (C) The woman doesn't ask when he has been to the movies.
9. (C) The question asks the woman to rate how Anne plays. The woman replies that she plays well. (A) The question does not ask how often she plays. (B) The question does not ask where she plays.
10. (C) The woman is asking how the man found the mistake. He replies with the method he used to find it. (A) assumes that it was the man's fault and he is apologizing, but the question doesn't ask who is at fault. (B) The question doesn't ask the severity of the mistake.
11. (A) The question asks for the age of the woman's son; the woman replies with his age. (B) The question doesn't ask for the height of the boy. (C) This answers the question, 'Who does the boy look like?'
12. (C) The woman wants to know if the man will go for lunch with her on Sunday; the man replies that he is unable to because he already has plans on Sunday. (A) The question doesn't ask what he would like to eat. (B) answers if they have already eaten and if he liked the food.
13. (B) The man wants to know what John's profession is. The woman tells the man the job John does. (A) answers where John lives. (C) answers what type of house he lives in.
14. (B) The woman inquires whether she has had a call from someone. The man replies that no one called her. (A) The question didn't ask if the man had called the woman. (C) The question doesn't ask for the man to call the woman.
15. (A) The man asks whether the woman recognizes the keys. The woman does, and she tells the man who they belong to. (B) The question doesn't ask whether the keys can be used in a lock. (C) The man doesn't ask for the woman to get new keys.
16. (B) The woman wants the man to listen to her song. The man doesn't see a problem with it and agrees to listen. (A) The woman doesn't ask if the man has heard the song at a concert. (C) answers with his like for another male singer.
17. (A) The man is asking for permission to go earlier than he usually does. The woman's answer assumes she means yes. (B) uses the word 'early' to mean the time at which he arrives somewhere. (C) answers the time it would take to go somewhere.
18. (A) The woman asks for help as to where she should place the fruit and suggests two options. The man replies with the best place she should put it. (B) answers that the man has a preference between bags and boxes. (C) doesn't give which option is preferred.
19. (B) The man asks for the reason as to why Peter is late. The woman gives the reason for his lateness. (A) answers that he wasn't late, but from the question we know he is late. (C) answers how long he has been late for.
20. (C) The woman asks if she should turn the air-conditioning on. The man thinks he would like it on. (A) answers whether it should be on or not. (B) answers that it's already on, but the woman wouldn't ask if it was a good idea to turn it on if it was already on.
21. (C) The man asks if the woman would like to eat her food there or take it away with her. The woman replies that she'll stay there. (A) uses 'take-away' in its literal sense, that something should be removed. (B) replies with a question and asks the man what he thinks, but it is the woman's choice to make.
22. (B) This question asks for the time. The man replies the time at which it opens. (A) answers if the gallery is already open. (C) answers where the gallery is.
23. (B) This question asks if there is anything wrong with Cherie. The woman replies with the reason for her being upset. (A) answers if the woman was angry with Cherie. (C) answers where Cherie is.
24. (C) The woman is asking for advice about the best place to get the bus from. The man gives a particular place she can get it. (A) answers what time the bus leaves. (B) answers where the bus goes.

25. (B) This question asks for the mode of transport the woman used to get to school. The woman replies that she went by bike. (A) answers the question 'How are you doing?'. (C) answers the question 'How did you get on at school today?'.
26. (A) The woman is asking for the period of time that he has worked. The man answers when he started. (B) answers how long is needed before he finishes. (C) answers where he works in the company, in which job.
27. (C) The man is asking for the possibility to pay in that way. The woman says he is unable to pay that way, only by money in the form of notes or coins. (A) answers how she would pay. (B) offers change, but the man hasn't paid yet.
28. (A) The woman wants to know if the man would like to get some exercise and go running. The man replies with a suggestion as to where they could run, so it is assumed he wants to go. (B) answers a question about a distance to run. (C) answers a question about the number of races he has run.
29. (B) This question asks about time and when the woman usually eats. The woman cannot give a clear answer as she is not sure, because the time she gets home from work varies. (A) answers whether the woman thinks it is a good time to eat or not. (C) answers if the woman has already had food.
30. (C) The woman wants to know what type of personality Susan has: her qualities. The man says she is very thoughtful and kind. (A) uses the word 'like' to mean he wishes he could meet Susan. (B) answers using the word 'like' to mean that Susan enjoyed the present.
31. (B) This question asks for the particular place where the passport was. The woman informs the man exactly where it was. (A) answers if the woman has the passport. (C) answers where you can get a passport.

Listening – Part 3: Conversations
32. (D) There is heavy traffic because it is summertime and there is a lot of construction.
33. (B) The woman has a fear of public speaking; she says it's all mental and has nothing to do with the material.
34. (A) The man feels that the content is more important than the delivery.
35. (C) The man needs to find Meredith as she has the Knight file he wants.
36. (A) The man feels it's his fault because he's had the file for three days and hasn't looked at it.
37. (A) The man will manage by improvising and letting Meredith do all the talking.
38. (D) The interviewer's presence and technique made the man very nervous.
39. (C) The man has also got an outstanding academic record.
40. (A) The woman believes that it isn't just the interview which could get the man the job, but his school grades, application, and references.
41. (C) They are at an airport waiting in the area where the baggage comes round on a carousel.
42. (C) They have already decided to get some coffee, and she adds that she is sleepy to justify needing some caffeine.
43. (B) The man says it's a small thank you for the ride to the airport.
44. (A) A colleague gave her the name of the doctor.
45. (C) She suffers with insomnia.
46. (D) The woman gets an appointment on Friday at 2; therefore, according to the graphic, she is Ms Brown.
47. (B) She had a great day even though she worked 14 hours.
48. (C) Her boss let her sit in on a meeting, which shows she is preparing her for more responsibilities.
49. (A) The woman told her boss she liked a particular design and her boss bought lots of it.
50. (A) Ed leaves at 3.30 a.m. because he's been there since 7 a.m.
51. (D) She admires how he is equally a good father and good at his work.
52. (C) He says once she has found her routine she will have more energy for more things.
53. (C) The man has gotten used to her being late over the last few years.
54. (B) They are interested in turning her columns into a book.
55. (D) She has just got a job offer that she was not expecting; therefore, she can't believe her luck at first.
56. (A) Advertising would give him the opportunity to show his creativity and intelligence.
57. (C) He will be able to gain experience and build up a portfolio.
58. (A) The man would be suitable for an entry level position because of his lack of experience, but would like to be paid; therefore, according to the graphic, the first job would be ideal.
59. (C) Another man, Paul, is related to the boss.
60. (C) The woman thinks that Paul certainly has the edge.
61. (B) Paul is related to the boss, Cindy.
62. (A) The printer broke and he couldn't get his report.
63. (C) She thinks they are both being very immature.
64. (D) She says if the two of them don't pull their socks up it will annoy 'our' boss, so they work for the same person.
65. (C) He made it look good with his computer images.
66. (D) He was stretching the truth a bit on costs.
67. (B) They think the project could be at risk and ask how he could do such a thing.
68. (D) He had an accident involving dangerous equipment in the factory.
69. (A) She says that 'suing' the company didn't make him employee of the month.
70. (A) She says he needs to make an effort to get on well with everyone at work.

Listening – Part 4: Talks
71. (D) They could cause higher fares.
72. (C) The levels have been unseen since the late 1980s.
73. (C) Airlines will try to reduce the number of seats that they sell cheaply on the internet.
74. (C) A red Ford Taurus is blocking the entrance.
75. (A) The car needs to be moved to the parking lot on the east or west side of the building.
76. (B) They will have to call the towing company.
77. (A) Shopping is sales tax-free.
78. (D) Many shops will ship your purchases to you.

79. (C) They create items that reflect and contain human spirit.
80. (C) The talk lists different services.
81. (D) Even if a time hasn't been agreed, a service is expected to come in good time.
82. (A) If someone works on something and then it still isn't fixed, then this is unacceptable.
83. (A) The food for your body and brain cells is oxygen.
84. (B) It gives up carbon dioxide.
85. (C) Understanding the body can help protect against heart attacks.
86. (C) After 1982, new rules came into place.
87. (B) The Secretary of State has certain controls over the name you choose.
88. (D) They protect the rights which persons may have in relation to names or words.
89. (C) A number of events were mentioned apart from soccer.
90. (B) He had a great struggle against the high waves and terrible cold.
91. (D) Approximately 300 people represented 13 countries.
92. (B) They will be at the airport at 6.30, an hour before their flight at 7.30.
93. (B) There are many ways they could entertain themselves, but having a snack is not mentioned.
94. (C) Their flight takes off at 7.30 from New York to Greece and it is a nine-hour flight, therefore arriving at 16.30 NY time. If you add to this seven hours, which is the time difference, then you get 23.30.
95. (B) All animals adapt to their environments aided by classical conditioning.
96. (D) We learn to repeat acts which give good outcomes and avoid acts that bring punishment.
97. (C) Humans are classified as among higher animal groups.
98. (C) She is calling on behalf of Mr Samuels to cancel his meeting; therefore, she is his secretary.
99. (B) Mr Samuels is available on weekdays 9–11 a.m. except for Tuesday and Friday this week. Mr Jones has a dentist appointment on Thursday during that time, which means that Wednesday is the only option.
100. (B) There was no way of knowing that Mr Samuels would get sick, so they couldn't have let Mr Jones know any sooner.

Reading – Part 5: Incomplete Sentences

101 C. If you want to have a successful interview, you must make a good impression. 'Make a good/bad impression' is a phrase.
102 B. Tim was always helpful and cheerful with customers; therefore, he was declared employee of the month. 'Therefore' means 'for that reason'.
103 C. Lea did a thorough job on the advertising campaign; she didn't miss a single detail. 'Thorough' means 'detailed and careful'. The fact that she didn't miss a single detail shows that it was thorough.
104 A. Maureen gave a talk when she attended the conference last week. We need a subject and a verb, and the past simple is used for something that happened at a fixed time in the past. Options B and C: the subject is missing.
105 D. You can pay by card over the phone, or we can issue you with an invoice. We issue somebody with something; in this case, an invoice.
106 C. One of the main reasons people attend conferences is for the networking opportunities. 'Networking' means meeting people who could be useful in the future.
107 D. While hard work is important, so is spending time with family and friends. We use 'while' in this way to show contrast. Contrast can also be shown by 'in spite of', but it would be followed by a noun or a gerund.
108 C. The collective opinion of the delegates was that the conference was a great success. 'Collective' means 'involving a group of people'.
109 A. Did you hear that Mr Richards proposed a whole new corporate strategy at the meeting yesterday? Option C: the article is needed; 'a wholly new ...' Options B and D are not possible.
110 D. In regard to your inquiry, we have no vacancies at this time. We say 'in regard to' or 'with regard to' to introduce a topic. The other prepositions are wrong.
111 D. Trevor chose to be a lawyer because he likes the challenge. We use the word 'challenge' to refer to something difficult that tests your ability.
112 A. All parties were happy with the results of the meeting because it was a win-win situation. The phrase 'win-win situation' means that all parties benefited in some way.
113 A. A lot of insurance companies are under pressure to increase premiums to stay solvent. If a company stays solvent, it means that it is able to pay its debts.
114 B. The goals of the two CEOs were different, so it was not easy for them to reach a compromise which they were both happy with. We say 'to reach a compromise' when two parties settle their differences by making concessions. The other words do not collocate.
115 C. I thought the new delegate would be here this afternoon. Where is she? 'Would be' is used here to show that the delegate is not there.
116 A. After making some changes, both the productivity and the profits of the company increased. 'Productivity' is the rate at which a company produces goods or services, and that is usually judged in relation to the number of people and the time necessary to produce them.
117 C. This factory has the capacity to produce 10,000 smartphone devices per year. 'Capacity' is the total amount that something can produce.
118 C. I regret to inform you that your application for the job has not been successful. When we write a formal letter to announce something unpleasant to somebody, we say, 'I regret to inform you that ...'
119 D. I would suggest you check with personnel before buying the plane ticket. We can say, 'I would suggest checking ...' or 'I would suggest (that) you (should) check ...'
120 A. Leila is ambitious; I know she will rise to the top quickly. If somebody is ambitious, they have dreams about the future and they want to succeed in life.
121 C. After having worked as a senior executive for 20 years, Peter decided to retire. After having worked = After he had worked. This is an action that happened before the past simple (decided). The present perfect is wrong here because it is connected with the present.

122 B. Having worked for 10 years as an accountant, Tom suffered a burnout and decided to change careers. Burnout is the state of being mentally or physically tired because of overworking.
123 C. The company is doing so well that the chairman was smiley and cheerful during the meeting. The adjective 'cheerful' is correct here, 'smiley and cheerful'. The word 'and' is used to join words of the same word class.
124 C. It's not advisable to rent a commercial property in this area as the business rates will be very high. Business rates = the money that businesses are charged as tax for local services; they vary depending on the area.
125 A. I specifically asked you to be here by 8 a.m.! What is your excuse this time? After the verb 'ask', we use infinitive, so we say 'ask somebody to do something'.
126 A. The security guard was made redundant when the bank installed a new high-tech alarm system. If someone is made redundant, they lose their job because they are no longer needed. The collocation is 'make somebody redundant'.
127 C. Jennifer was one of only three candidates invited for an interview. We say 'invite somebody for an interview', then, if they are successful, they will be offered the job.
128 C. The first-aid seminar is obligatory; you must attend. If something is obligatory, you have to do it. 'Obligatory' is an adjective, and here we need an adjective after the verb 'is' to describe the first-aid seminar.
129 D. Alexander is a superb architect, but his fees are rather high so we gave the job to someone else. Architects, schools, etc., charge fees. So if you receive their services, you pay those fees.
130 A. It was rash of Judy to quit her job – she'll probably be sorry later. We say, 'It was rash of somebody to do something.' The adjective 'rash' means unwise, without thought of what might happen.

Reading – Part 6: Text Completion

131 C. I am sending this letter of complaint because of the service I received while traveling on your Flight 779 from Minneapolis to New York on September 19th. 'Complain' is a verb, so it is wrong here. 'A letter of complaint' is a letter we send to somebody to complain about something.
132 D. I had to ask four times and become quite agitated before the cabin crew would search for the meal which I had reason to believe was there. If somebody is 'agitated', they are nervous because of worry or fear that is difficult to control. Situations can be 'complicated'. 'Motivated' has a positive meaning, being determined because you really want to do something, and 'interrogated' means being asked questions.
133 A. You can understand my concern, I'm sure, because eating regular meals, made up of the right foods, is critical for managing this illness. John Baker is diabetic, so his diet can help him control the disease. Therefore, the only answer that makes sense is 'critical', which means 'of the greatest importance'. If something is 'detrimental', it causes harm or damage.
134 C. Regrettably, I'm not sure I would feel confident traveling with you in the future. John Baker was not happy about the way he was treated by the cabin crew, as he had to ask for his special meal four times. To him, it 'seemed like unnecessary rudeness'.
135 C. More than $160m will be spent on music and video downloads in the USA this year, according to a poll. A poll is a study in which people are asked for their opinions about something.
136 D. … And digital spending will continue to soar, reaching $700m a year by the end of the decade, according to USA Music and Video Streaming's latest report. If prices soar, they rise very quickly to a high level.
137 C. But CD and DVD spending has slowed, with the overall USA music and video market down 2.9%, to $4bn this year. We use the adjective 'overall' to show that we are talking about a situation in general.
138 C. On the other hand, sales of vinyl have increased as records make a spectacular resurgence. 'On the other hand' is correct here because it starts the sentence by introducing something contrasting.
139 C. As you know, we are expecting a visit from health inspectors this week. When we start a letter or email, we usually say why we are writing. Option A is about a change, so it is wrong. Option B refers to the previous week, while the rest of the text refers to a future visit.
140 D. It is essential that you carry out your usual cleaning and sanitation procedures with the utmost care this week. 'Carry out' means to do or complete something in the way you have been told to do it.
141 B. Do not take short cuts. A short cut is a quicker way of doing something in order to save time or effort. The other options do not make sense.
142 A. Make sure meats are kept on the upper shelf in the refrigeration unit, because the temperature is not high enough on the lower shelf. Make sure = ensure. It's a collocation.
143 B. This is to inform you that we have carefully reviewed your estimate for the parking lot refurbishing. If you review something, you think about it again in order to make a decision. And, according to this email, they have reviewed this case carefully.
144 A. We are unable to sign this contract immediately, however, as final approval of expenditures of this nature must come from the head office in New York. Because = as, so option D is wrong. 'Despite' and 'although' are used with different syntax and are never immediately followed by a comma. 'However', which shows contrast, is followed by a comma.
145 B. We expect to receive approval or disapproval within the next 30 days. 'Within' means 'not further than this period of time'. We can say 'on Friday' or 'on the 14th of June'. 'Since' is used with the present perfect to show when an action started.
146 C. If we may be of any assistance in the meantime, please feel free to contact this office. We say we contact a place or a person; no preposition is used. We also say, 'feel free to do something'.

Reading – Part 7: Reading Comprehension
Questions 147–149

147. The correct answer is (A); the advertisement says Anthony's Pier is famous for its fine seafood and tasty American dishes.
148. The correct answer is (C); the advertisement gives a telephone number, postal address, and fax number and, although there's a web address, there's no email address.

Answer Explanations

149. The correct answer is (B); the advert says that it is open on Sunday from 12 p.m. to 10 p.m. and they serve dinner all day.

Questions 150–151

150. The correct answer is (C); the notice is about a careers exhibition organized by the career services of Florida State University and is most likely to be found on a college campus.

151. The correct answer is (A); the notice informs people about the Careers Expo which is being held at the Holiday Inn Select, 3535 Ulmerton Road.

Questions 152–154

152. The correct answer is (C); in the announcement, towards the top, it says under 'apply' to click here!, showing this is a link on a website.

153. The correct answer is (C); under 'Qualifications', excellent knowledge of written and spoken English is needed.

154. The correct answer is (A); the research will specifically be about probability (pure and/or applied).

Questions 155–157

155. The correct answer is (D); the insert outlines the physical demands that must be met by anyone applying for the job.

156. The correct answer is (B); the employee would be required to consistently work from high places, such as roofs, ceilings, and ladders.

157. The correct answer is (A); the insert talks about having to drive to different places, having to work on roofs and ladders as well as with heavy materials and equipment.

Questions 158–160

158. The correct answer is (A); it is the first time a sitting president will have appeared in public with the 72-year-old Buddhist leader.

159. The correct answer is (B); the religious leader is 72 years old.

160. The correct answer is (D); the President hopes that the objectors would get to know the religious leader as the President sees him – as a spiritual leader and someone who wants peace.

Questions 161–163

161. The correct answer is (A); the notice apologizes for any inconvenience to those with offices on Level 4.

162. The correct answer is (C); they will be refurbished between 3 p.m. on Friday and 1 p.m. on Monday.

163. The correct answer is (A); people will still be able to use the restrooms on Level 1 and Level 2.

Questions 164–166

164. The correct answer is (B); the time on the ticket is 1:30 p.m. – lunchtime.

165. The correct answer is (C); three portions of chocolate cake and three drinks were ordered.

166. The correct answer is (D); the bill includes sparkling water and orange juice, sales tax of $2.86, and chocolate cake.

Questions 167–168

167. The correct answer is (B); the Republican Party presidential candidates are given as Mr Kiuliani and Mr Somney in the first paragraph. They are described as 'The ex-Austin, TX, mayor' and 'the former Florida governor', presumably in the order of the names given in the previous paragraph.

168. The correct answer is (A); it's a news report, following a televised debate.

Questions 169–172

169. The correct answer is (B); the email was sent to Anna and copies were sent to Bill, Jason, Maria, and Jodie.

170. The correct answer is (A); according to the email, the meeting is due to start at 9:30 sharp.

171. The correct answer is (D); the email has been sent by Mark and his email address ends with '@rg_inc.org', suggesting that www.rg_inc.org is the website

172. The correct answer is (D), as Mr Stewart is going to inform them about the new advertising regulations.

Questions 173–175

173. The correct answer is (D); the card refers to the instructions for an emergency landing.

174. The correct answer is (A); aisle lights will guide people to the nearest exit.

175. The correct answer is (B); you need to have your life vest to inflate when you have left the plane.

Questions 176-180

176. The correct answer is (D); the web page says that with interactive lessons and the option to work with other people, you'll be able to learn how you want, go at your own pace, or follow the weekly syllabus.

177. The correct answer is (D), the course covers the differences between SXHTML and SHTML, text manipulation and lists, images, tables, and frames.

178. The correct answer is (C); the previous sentence mentions that you can learn the way you want; that is, at your own pace or in accordance with the weekly syllabus.

179. The correct answer is (A); Alistair says he stumbled across the website and thought of her.

180. The correct answer is (B); the email begins 'Hi Josephine', is informal and friendly, and concludes with 'Keep in touch'.

Questions 181–185

181. The correct answer is (B); according to the email, Terry will have to sit at the registration desk and answer questions.

182. The correct answer is (B); Mabel asks Terry to let her know if he received the email and if the times are fine with him.

183. The correct answer is (A); according to the attachment, registration on Tuesday morning is from 8 a.m. to 10 a.m.

184. The correct answer is (A); the Exhibit Hall opens 2.00 p.m.–5.00 p.m. and the Afternoon Technical Sessions are 4.30 p.m.–7.00 p.m.

185. The correct answer is (D); the Morning Technical Sessions are 10.15 a.m.–12.00 p.m., 1 hour and 45 minutes.

Questions 186–190

186. The correct answer is (B); the accident happened on the 29th of December, and this letter was sent on the 18th of January, approximately two weeks later.

187. The correct answer is (B); the letter informs Timothy that a police report is needed to determine who is at fault for the accident.

188. The correct answer is (A); the previous sentence refers to the claim received, while the following sentence mentions the police report, which is an example of the documentation needed.

189. The correct answer is (D); they have no time to spare, as sending the police report to the Claims Appraiser is urgent.
190. The correct answer is (C); Mr Bancroft is a claims appraiser so is most likely to work in the Claims Department.
Questions 191–195
191. The correct answer is (C); the intermittent bell is the least serious. It is only local to the lift area and only Security has to be informed.
192. The correct answer is (A); the klaxon horn indicates a laboratory alarm has been activated.
193. The correct answer is (A); if there's a continuously sounding fire bell, staff are expected to follow the emergency procedures detailed in the safety regulations.
194. The correct answer is (C); the memo is addressed to 'all employees' and has been issued to clarify uncertainty about the procedures, which was experienced the week before.
195. The correct answer is (D); 'alarms will be tested on a weekly basis'.
Questions 196–200
196. The correct answer is (B); the new store is the Pine Avenue branch of Bordering Books.
197. The correct answer is (A); it opens with 'Dear neighbor' and the address at the top of the letter is 23 Pine Avenue.
198. The correct answer is (A); on the second floor there is the signature Bordering Cafe coffee shop.
199. The correct answer is (A); Bob knows that Jim enjoys reading, so when Jim suggests meeting at the cafe in Bordering Bookshop, Bob is certain that Jim will want to buy a book again.
200. The correct answer is (C); the coupon is good for one hot drink and one pastry.

TEST 3

Listening – Part 1: Photographs
1. (C) The man holding the video camera is pointing his finger with his left hand. (D) Both men in the picture have straight faces. (A) The men aren't acting, and because they are holding the filming equipment, they are the ones behind the scenes. (B) Neither man is holding a camera for photography.
2. (B) In the picture, the man on the left is giving an award to the other man and at the same time shaking his hand congratulating him. (A) Only the man on the left has glasses on his face. (C) The microphone, a small black device to speak to a crowd, is situated on the left. (D) The men are not sitting around a table discussing topics with anyone.
3. (A) In the picture, there are two people in the front row, one of whom is a woman. (B) Around the two people at the front there are a number of seats with no one sitting on them. (C) They appear to be in a hall; other people in the crowd have recording equipment and cameras. (D) We cannot tell whether a man is speaking.
4. (D) In the picture, there are three people; the doctor is the one wearing a mask, sitting down and writing. (A) The patient is the one being treated, he is sitting on the left and has no mask on his face. (B) The doctor is not speaking to anyone, but focusing on what he is writing. He is looking down. (C) The nurse is the woman on the right; she is wearing a nurse's uniform and she is standing.
5. (C) The airplane is not in motion; it has the steps at the side and people are getting off. (A) They are getting off the plane rather than getting on/boarding. (B) The airplane is still on the ground and the people are outside of the plane. (D) The picture shows the outside of the plane, with blue sky at the top.
6. (D) In the picture, the girl on the right has a bottle of drink in her left hand. (A) The picture shows three people: a man is interviewing a boy and a girl. (B) The boy is wearing clothes with long sleeves, including a jumper. (C) The man on the left has a microphone in one hand and some pieces of paper in the other.

Listening – Part 2: Question-Response
7. (B) The question asks if the evaluations have been completed. The woman replies that they have nearly been done. (A) answers how many questions there were. (C) answers how much time it took filling out the evaluation.
8. (C) The woman indicates that she knows the man has been in Honolulu. The man confirms he has and would like to go back.(A) answers "Will you be going to Honolulu?". (B) answers "How long did you stay in Honolulu?".
9. (A) The man inquires how he can get his money back. The woman advises him how he can. (B) answers how the presentation went. (C) answers where the presentation is.
10. (B) The woman wants to know the time the brunch will start. The man thinks he knows and gives a time. (A) The question doesn't ask about a schedule. (C) The question doesn't ask what food there will be.
11. (A) The man suggests a restaurant Paul mentioned. The woman agrees that it is a good idea. (B) suggests that the man will cook instead. (C) is an irrelevant question.
12. (C) The woman wants to know about the time someone will leave. The man replies that the time will be before lunchtime. (A) answers where her flight gate will be. (B) answers which transport she will use.
13. (B) The man wants to know when the work will be finished. The woman gives an estimated time – around spring. (A) answers how it will look when it's finished. (C) speaks about cost.
14. (A) The woman is curious as to where the couch came from. The man informs her where he bought it. (B) answers what the new couch is for. (C) speaks about meeting a woman.
15. (B) The man asks for help to find the nearest bakery. The woman tells him the address of the nearest one. (A) answers if the bakery is open or closed. (C) answers what type of food is sold at the bakery.
16. (C) The woman is unsure of the man's name and gives options of what she thinks it could be. The man replies that neither of her options is correct; it is in fact another name. (A) answers what job he does. (B) says that the man wants to do the other man's job.
17. (A) The man wants to know if the woman has eaten any of the cookies. The woman replies that she hasn't, but she has been told they are very nice. (B) answers as

if the man has offered the woman to eat the cookies. (C) answers as if the man has inquired about something being completed.

18. (A) The woman reminds the man of the consequences of late rent. The man already knows and says that he is always on time with the payment. (B) answers if he thinks he pays too much. (C) answers how he pays the rent.

19. (B) The man offers to get the woman a drink as he is already getting up. The woman would like a drink and accepts his offer politely. (A) The question doesn't ask if the woman would like to go away from where they are. (C) answers as if the man hasn't responded correctly to her question.

20. (A) The woman inquires whether a degree is needed to be eligible. The man says that a degree is favorable. (B) answers the question when something will begin. (C) The question only mentions one point, and the answer suggests that two things are acceptable.

21. (B) The man inquires whether the woman has looked at poverty rates. The man has, and he replies with the information he knows. (A) The question doesn't require an amount in money. (C) speaks in the present. The question refers to the past.

22. (B) The woman requires assistance with phoning somewhere far away. The man tells the woman how. (A) The question doesn't mention where and whom the woman wants to call. (C) The answer doesn't require directions or distance times.

23. (A) The man wants to know what train the other woman will get on. The woman thinks she knows and gives the information. (B) The question doesn't ask if she will do something and doesn't inquire when she will do it. (C) The question doesn't require an opinion on the conditions of the train station.

24. (C) The woman wants to know when her internet will work. The man confirms that it will be by the end of the month. (A) answers in the past tense. (B) associates the word 'connection' with trains, a conductor being on a train. The connection here means the use of the internet service.

25. (A) The man wants to know if the woman was able to make an appointment. The woman explains that she tried to but was unable to because there were no places. (B) suggests she doesn't ever want to make an appointment. (C) associates the word 'manage' with 'management', a boss.

26. (B) The woman wants to find out if anyone has left her any messages. The man replies that only one person has and he gives the message. (A) answers as if the woman misunderstood him. (C) answers as if the woman requires the man to do something.

27. (A) The man wants to know what the weather will be like. The woman hopes the weather will be good so she can go out. (B) confuses the word 'sun' with 'son', and says that a man has a daughter. (C) answers as if the weather is something to be decided on.

28. (C) The woman asks the man if he would like a ride to work. The man thinks it's a good idea as they are near each other anyway. (A) confuses 'car pool' with 'swimming pool'. (B) answers how busy the roads will be.

29. (C) The man wants to know about the woman and asks her preferences. The woman informs the man which she likes best. (A) answers the question "What do you like to do?". (B) answers with the woman's opinion on what everyone else does.

30. (A) The woman wants to know what the temperature was like in summer in Miami. The man confirms that it was hot and how he coped. (B) answers when he thinks he will return from Miami. (C) answers what kind of people there are in Miami.

31. (B) The man asks for advice about a choice he wants to make. The woman suggests what she thinks the best idea would be. (A) associates the phrase 'come out' with literally going outside. Here it means when it is available. (C) answers as if someone had asked for a particular time.

Listening – Part 3: Conversations

32. (B) It's two hours from the airport to the center, plus check-in and traveling time, thus making it longer to fly.

33. (D) The man would need a rental car to get to the center.

34. (C) He will be able to get money back.

35. (C) They are complaining to the manager of a restaurant, as a server is being mentioned.

36. (A) They waited very long for their orders, and the orders were incorrect.

37. (C) The meal will be on the house, and she will also give them free cheesecake.

38. (A) He asks why they should hire her.

39. (A) She tells him about her previous experience and positive attitude.

40. (B) She is happy to dedicate herself to something she loves.

41. (D) She isn't going to work today because she has a fever.

42. (B) She will meet Colleen about the curriculum changes when she's back on her feet.

43. (B) He tells her that he will inform everyone not to bother her.

44. (A) They are parents discussing how their respective children are doing at university.

45. (C) He worries that his son won't be able to make a living.

46. (D) She thinks that the man should agree to let him find his own path.

47. (C) Her previous one crashed.

48. (B) The woman is looking for a laptop, she is a basic user, and she is on a budget.

49. (B) He wants to know what she uses it for, to give her the best one.

50. (D) He introduces himself and welcomes her to the company.

51. (A) It's the woman's first day at work and she's trying to get used to everything, which can be a bit overwhelming.

52. (B) He says it's surprisingly good. He likes the lasagne.

53. (D) The woman wants to buy a particular book from the bookstore.

54. (B) She will go to the other store for the specific book she wants.

55. (C) It's the only option for her to get the book.

56. (C) He says he wants to sleep in, travel, and finish the home repairs.

57. (D) She says they have 10 more years before they retire.

58. (A) Since he often has time to take a nap on the couch, this means that he would have free time to do something else if he wanted to.
59. (C) Since she is told that the doctor is booked for the entire hour before her 3.30 appointment, we conclude she got there around 2.30.
60. (C) She was in the area and didn't want to return home for such a short time.
61. (A) She'll go to a local coffee shop and read her book.
62. (C) He went off without his laptop last time.
63. (B) He will be in a meeting so won't be able to phone until later.
64. (A) They are married; she addresses him as "dear".
65. (B) The man is on the phone talking the woman through the problem with her computer.
66. (A) Her computer is not plugged into an electrical socket on the wall.
67. (D) The man tells the woman it was an easy mistake to make, so he's understanding.
68. (C) He is a bit under the weather; that is, ill.
69. (C) The meeting has been canceled; they'll sort out a day for the following week to hold it.
70. (B) Susan was willing to help him, so in the future he must help her back.

Listening – Part 4: Talks
71. (A) They are addressed as future entrepreneurs.
72. (C) The fourth point should have to do with the competition; therefore, other coffee houses.
73. (B) If you're a high-end retailer, they will support your business.
74. (D) An ice storm hit the state and took out the electricity.
75. (B) This winter, it is best to head south instead of north for snow.
76. (A) During the winter, there are likely to be snowstorms, spells of mild weather, as well as dry days, while in the summer there can be a heatwave. Thus, the weather can be variable.
77. (B) He assures them that the first lecture will be brief.
78. (D) It has created many new companies and thousands of jobs.
79. (A) It will become the heart of a large scientific and engineering community.
80. (C) It's an easy meal that can be made in no time.
81. (B) You need to toast pine nuts over a medium heat.
82. (D) A dish that includes salad and vegetables.
83. (C) It advises on simple points that are important when making a speech to an audience.
84. (D) Glance at their notes infrequently.
85. (A) If you make an error, correct it and move on.
86. (A) 'Working people' is one of several examples that follow of people who need to have flexible schedules when it comes to education.
87. (D) Classes from the internet in the comfort of your home are offered, but not group ones.
88. (B) There are weekday evening classes, weekend classes, and classes via the internet; therefore, most people would be accommodated.
89. (D) The following sentence mentions a mechanical problem that has been taken care of; therefore, patience was needed throughout this process.
90. (A) The plane is going to Tampa, Florida.
91. (B) The flight is full, so you should only board when your zone is called.
92. (C) He is just leaving the State Fair.
93. (D) She works for Channel 8 and hopes he'll tell the viewers about the fair.
94. (B) She is most interested in knowing the tastiest food he ate.
95. (A) At Stowe Hall, where they usually eat.
96. (B) The meeting will end at 5.30, an hour earlier than the usual 6.30.
97. (D) The sessions are focused on different aspects of teaching, plus the attendees are expected to head for the airport tomorrow, indicating that it could be an overseas event.
98. (D) They should wait for the intermission to leave, unless it's an emergency.
99. (B) The bathrooms are located to the right of the entrance and down the hall.
100. (C) The actors will be in the lobby for autographs and pictures.

Reading – Part 5: Incomplete Sentences
101 B. Jerry was surprised that the projects were completed so quickly. 'So' can be followed by an adjective or an adverb. We can say, for example, 'He is so quick!' or 'He walks so quickly!'. 'Too' adds a negative meaning.
102 C. The company must hire 50 new employees by September 15th next year. 'Must' is a modal verb, and after modal verbs we use the infinitive without 'to'. If we use the infinite 'hire', it usually refers to a present or future situation. If we use the perfect infinitive 'have hired', it usually refers to a past situation. 'Be hired' is passive, so it does not make sense here.
103 A. Unfortunately, due to the company's financial problems, they will have to severely cut back on staff. If we 'cut back on' or 'cut down on' something, we reduce the number or amount of it.
104 C. Personal phone calls cannot be made from the office telephone. We need the passive voice here. We could say the same thing using the active voice, 'People/Staff cannot make personal phone calls ...'. We can also say, 'Personal phone calls aren't allowed ... '.
105 B. Jack said that he couldn't read his colleague's note because his handwriting was illegible. If something is illegible, it is difficult or impossible to read.
106 B. We cleaned the restaurant all night in order to satisfy all the health code regulations. If something 'satisfies the regulations', it meets the requirements (it is what it is expected to be).
107 C. Rarely does he invest in the stock market. If a sentence starts with a negative adverb such as 'rarely', we use inversion. The word order is the same as the word order we use in questions, but it is not a question. So, we say 'Rarely/Hardly/Scarcely/Never does somebody do something ...'.
108 A. Unlike our competitors, our store is open 24 hours a day for your convenience. 'Unlike' here means 'in contrast with'.
109 A. If your subscription to *USA Today* expires, you may renew it online. We renew a subscription when it expires, and we usually pay money to renew it.

110 B. Kate Fox has been appointed to the board of directors. If someone is appointed to a position, it means that this person is chosen to do this job.
111 A. All the sponsors will be acknowledged by the organization president. Active voice: 'The president will acknowledge all sponsors.' Passive voice: 'All the sponsors will be acknowledged by the organization president.'
112 D. In response to consumer demand, our products will be packaged using recycled products. 'In response to' means 'in answer to'. We could also use 'because of'.
113 D. This state-of-the-art computer comes with a two-year guarantee of quality. When we buy something such as a device, we get a guarantee, so if it breaks down, we can return it.
114 C. So far, everyone who's heard the news about Gerry's appointment as head of sales is thrilled about it. We can say, 'thrilled about' or 'thrilled by'. The word 'news' is uncountable, so it is singular.
115 A. Establishing a good working relationship between management and the workforce is a challenge. When we join two things/people with the word 'between', we use the word 'and'. So, we say 'between A and B'.
116 B. Productivity has fallen dramatically during the last three years and is struggling to catch up. 'Catch up' means to 'keep pace with' or 'to increase so that it can reach the required level.'
117 D. The conference's turnout has nearly doubled in the last few years. We can also say, 'The conference's turnout is now twice as much as it was a few years ago.'
118 C. The regional vice president is in charge of conducting company evaluations. We can also say 'The regional vice president is responsible for conducting ...' .
119 B. Although my office is nicely decorated, it is too small for my filing cabinet and desk chair. 'And' here connects the two noun phrases: filing cabinet and desk chair.
120 A. This new tablet was very expensive, so please handle it with care. We can say, 'handle it with care' or 'handle it carefully'.
121 B. Ms Barton's assistant will explain the details of the new mail policy. The word 'assistant' is used in this context. A manager or somebody who is in a high position in a company or organization usually has an assistant.
122 C. Whenever possible, Mr Brown tries to visit all of the company's offices. 'Whenever' refers to time and that is why it is the correct answer. 'Whenever' means, 'every time it is possible'.
123 D. Should Mr Arnold replace Mr Dendler, his salary would be doubled. This means: 'If Mr Arnold replaced Mr Dendler, his salary would be doubled' = 'Were Mr Arnold to replace Mr Dendler, his salary would be doubled.'
124 A. Mr Cook is solely responsible for any debts the company may incur. 'Solely' means 'only, exclusively'. Here, we use an adverb to modify the adjective 'responsible'. The word 'lonely' is an adjective that means that somebody feels sad because he/she does not have somebody with them.
125 C. The conference room he selected for the meeting was on the sixth floor. The long noun phrase 'The conference room (that) he selected for the meeting' is the subject of the verb 'was'. Within this noun phrase, there is a relative clause where the relative pronoun is omitted.
126 A. The two electrical companies announced plans for a joint venture. A venture is a new activity, usually in business, which involves risk or uncertainty.
127 C. Henry was promoted last week from conductor to supervisor. It is an example of passive voice. They promoted Henry from conductor to supervisor. A, B, and D are in the active voice.
128 B. The manager ordered new uniforms for the staff last month. 'Staff' means personnel, the people who work in a company.
129 A. Every once in a while, Patrick treats his customers to a free dessert. 'Once in a while' or 'every once in a while' is a phrase which means occasionally, not very often.
130 B. Please list your email address and WhatsApp number with all correspondence. Correspondence is communication other than face to face, usually by exchanging mails or letters.

Reading – Part 6: Text Completion
131 A. Once again, truth is stranger than fiction, and this enthralling cat-and-mouse game was <u>inspired</u> by the exploits of audacious Frank W Abagnale Jr, known as the Skywayman. 'Truth is stranger than fiction' is used to say that things that actually happen are often more surprising than stories that are invented. So, this story was based on and inspired by Frank's adventurous life.
132 C. ... who patiently pursued him <u>around</u> the world while developing a curious surrogate-father/son relationship with the daring identity thief. We can say 'around the world' or 'all over the world'.
133 C. ... it's a cockeyed version of the American dream: an ingenious, jet-setting grifter who scammed bad checks in 50 states and 26 countries, bilking banks of $2.5 million, <u>yet</u> he's still haunted by the sins of his parents which fractured his family. 'Yet' means 'despite that'. 'Although' is followed by subject + verb.
134 D. After serving five years, Abagnale was released from prison on the condition that he teach law enforcement how to prevent fraud. <u>Now he has his own security firm and lectures at the FBI Academy.</u> Abagnale was released from prison on the condition that he would help the police, who deal with law enforcement. So now he has a job related to this; he works or cooperates with the police (B is wrong); he does not commit crime (A and C are wrong).
135 C. Most people plan financially long-term, but they don't have a long-term physical plan. They plan for retirement, but they don't prepare for what I call physical "re-firement" in the <u>later</u> years in life. 'In the later years' is a phrase that means 'when someone is older'.
136 B. In 11th grade, I decided to never let myself get out of <u>shape</u> again. It's too much work. 'Out of shape' is a phrase that means 'not physically strong'.
137 A. People aren't used to focusing <u>on</u> their muscles the way I make them focus. The verb 'focus' is followed by the preposition 'on'.
138 B. If you do everything correctly, you'll have better results in a shorter <u>period</u> of time. We say 'a period of time'; the other words do not collocate.

139 C. I'm glad you are all here today. Obviously, the better communication we can have about issues that worry you, the easier it is for us to respond to problems. 'Obviously' means 'clearly'. Here, the speaker wants to say that it is clear that the better communication they can have about issues that worry them, the easier it is for them to respond to problems.
140 B. Our job is to identify problems and deal with them. And the best way to do so is in the spirit of cooperation. The words 'to do so' refer to the previous words 'identify problems' and 'deal with them'. The previous sentence also refers to problem-solving.
141 B. But we'll continue to work hard to help you, because by helping our governors, we really help our people. We say 'continue to do something' or 'continue doing something'. The other words are not followed by an infinitive; they are followed by a noun or adjective/adverb phrase, e.g., 'maintain the good standards' or 'remain silent'.
142 A. Yesterday, in my toast, I said the war on drugs goes on, and it does. I wish I could report otherwise, but that's not a true assessment of the world. After 'wish' we use 'could' when the subject remains the same, 'I wish I could do something'.
143 A. Absentee landlords were a highly significant issue in the history of Ireland. 'Significant' means important or noticeable. The word 'considerable' means large or important enough to have an effect on something, but it does not collocate well with the word 'issue'. 'Eminent' has a positive meaning only, and it usually describes people or a positive quality.
144 D. Seized land was given to English nobles and soldiers, some of whom rented it out to Irishmen while they remained residents of England. When we use the structure 'some of whom', we cannot use 'who'. This is because of the preposition 'of'.
145 C. In the years following the Irish Potato Famine, the land issue with the Irish Land League's Land War had become extremely important in Ireland. 'In the years following' = 'in the years that (had) followed'.
146 A. The land issue was one of the historic factors that resulted in Ireland's troubled history to this day. We say 'resulted in something' or 'caused something'.

Reading – Part 7: Reading Comprehension
Questions 147–149
147. The correct answer is (C); if you come with a party of eight people or more, they will throw in a free dessert for everyone.
148. The correct answer is (B); it's a family restaurant, with satellite sports TV and a great kids' menu.
149. The correct answer is (D); the restaurant is open seven days a week for lunch, dinner, late-night, and take-out. It doesn't offer breakfast.
Questions 150–153
150. The correct answer is (B); the price had dropped \$1.75, to \$50.49, making the original price \$52.24.
151. The correct answer is (A); experts were only predicting an increase of 325,000 barrels.
152. The correct answer is (D); reports were released by the federal Energy Information Administration (EIA).
153. The correct answer is (C); the inventory results are higher than analysts' expectations in the case of crude oil and motor gasoline stocks, while heating oil and diesel fuel are lower than analysts' predictions.
Questions 154–157
154. The correct answer is (B); they enjoy a greater variety of assignments.
155. The correct answer is (C); the leaflet says a major drawback is the uncertainty of work, and therefore income.
156. The correct answer is (D); if freelancers choose to pay for professional services, it can mean significant out-of-pocket expenses passed on to the client, which is usually not welcome.
157. The correct answer is (A); paragraph 1 outlines the benefits of freelancing and paragraphs 2 and 3 outline the drawbacks.
Questions 158–160
158. The correct answer is (A); if you are primarily remembered for your interview attire, you have made an error in judgment.
159. The correct answer is (C); appropriate attire supports your image as a person who takes the interview process seriously and understands the nature of the industry in which you are trying to become employed.
160. The correct answer is (C); the previous sentence mentions that you shouldn't dress for a social event, an example of which is a party or a date.
Questions 161–163
161. The correct answer is (A); she has played at outside back, forward, and outside midfield.
162. The correct answer is (C); she is one of only four Boilermakers to have played in over 80 matches.
163. The correct answer is (D); she broke the record for matches played in the first round of the All-Big Ten Tournament.
Questions 164–167
164. The correct answer is (B); you should be ready to support past career accomplishments with specific information targeted toward the company's needs.
165. The correct answer is (D); tip 2 suggests role-playing (rehearsing).
166. The correct answer is (B); encourage the interviewer to share information about the company.
167. The correct answer is (D); paying attention to your surroundings, including office furniture, will help you tailor your presentation.
Questions 168–169
168. The correct answer is (A); the card advertises a hotel in Miami Beach.
169. The correct answer is (B); it describes the accommodation, atmosphere, and service to encourage people to try the hotel.
Questions 170–171
170. The correct answer is (B); the jobless rate fell to its lowest in 33 years.
171. The correct answer is (D); the report speaks about jobs, inflation, and interest rates.
Questions 172–173
172. The correct answer is (B); the notice is to attract businesses looking for office space.
173. The correct answer is (B); if your goal is to find the right office, make sure to avoid costly mistakes.

Answer Explanations

Questions 174–175

174. The correct answer is (C); she asks the man to call Mr Brown to reschedule a business meeting she has with him.

175. The correct answer is (A); she will be getting to the office in a taxi, already arranged for her by Mr Dean, so there is no need for someone else to pick her up.

Questions 176–180

176. The correct answer is (C); the paragraph refers to the success of the school, its modern facilities, and comprehensive curriculum.

177. The correct answer is (A); the responsibilities include developing and maintaining an in-school recruiting program, rather than external recruitment for coaching staff.

178. The correct answer is (A); the information is given in more detail in his resume, which is attached to the letter.

179. The correct answer is (B); although he is in the process of obtaining a Virginia license, he will not have a secondary education endorsement on the license, which is preferred.

180. The correct answer is (C); after he took over as coach, the school won many events.

Questions 181–185

181. The correct answer is (D); Josh has to meet his deadline.

182. The correct answer is (C); Kelly seems not to be on such a tight work schedule as the man; therefore, she has time to spare on other things.

183. The correct answer is (B); she sent an email with an attachment.

184. The correct answer is (A); the man felt sorry for them because he thought they couldn't afford two meals.

185. The correct answer is (B); at the end of the story, the punch line says that she is waiting for the teeth.

Questions 186–190

186. The correct answer is (D); he only wants to work in Spanish-speaking countries.

187. The correct answer is (D); the previous sentence mentions the qualifications needed for the position, which would justify Robert mentioning his lack of experience.

188. The correct answer is (A); he tells her to 'Best avoid my kitchen duties'.

189. The correct answer is (C); caring for the old, as he volunteered at a senior citizen living center.

190. The correct answer is (B); community development covers broad issues, including economic assistance, human rights, healthcare, cultural heritage, environment, and women's issues.

Questions 191–192

191. The correct answer is (B); the class has discussed unemployment in the context of gender and race during the course.

192. The correct answer is (C); they are writing their final papers, which are usually near the end of the school year.

193. The correct answer is (A); the email refers to a 'quantitative survey', which usually involves a large number or selected groups of people.

194. The correct answer is (C); the number of unemployed people (6.8 million) was almost unchanged in December, and the unemployment rate was held at 4.5 per cent.

195. The correct answer is (B); adult women are 3.9 per cent, compared with adult men at 4.0 per cent, Hispanics at 4.9 per cent, and teenagers at 15.2 per cent.

Questions 196–200

196. The correct answer is (A); below the e-ticket/voucher heading, the invoice number is 471016.

197. The correct answer is (C); receiving comments is the best means they have for checking the quality of the hotels.

198. The correct answer is (A); the letter advises him to print it out and take it with him to the airport.

199. The correct answer is (C);'I didn't bother with the gym membership'.

200. The correct answer is (B); the baggage allowance is two pieces with the total weight of 20kg.

TEST 1

LISTENING – Section 1

Part 1: 1.C 2.C 3.A 4.D 5.C 6.A
Part 2: 7.B 8.C 9.C 10.A 11.C 12.B 13.C 14.C 15.A 16.C 17.B 18.C 19.C 20.A 21.C 22.A 23.B 24.A 25.C 26.C 27.B 28.C 29.B 30.B 31.C
Part 3: 32.B 33.C 34.A 35.C 36.B 37.A 38.D 39.B 40.C 41.B 42.C 43.B 44.D 45.A 46.D 47.B 48.C 49.B 50.C 51.B 52.C 53.C 54.C 55.A 56.D 57.B 58.D 59.A 60.A 61.B 62.A 63.C 64.D 65.C 66.B 67.B 68.A 69.A 70.D
Part 4: 71.C 72.D 73.A 74.C 75.A 76.D 77.C 78.A 79.C 80.B 81.A 82.C 83.C 84.D 85.A 86.C 87.B 88.C 89.A 90.B 91.C 92.A 93.D 94.C 95.B 96.A 97.A 98.B 99.D 100.C

Vocabulary Development for Test 1
(Reading parts 5-6)
Ex.A.: 1.A 2.C 3.B 4.A
Ex.B.: 5.B 6.A 7.A
Ex.C.: 8. incensed 9. marginal 10. enlightenment

READING – Section 2

Part 5: 101.D 102.C 103.B 104.C 105.D 106.D 107.A 108.A 109.D 110.C 111.D 112.A 113.B 114.C 115.B 116.B 117.A 118.B 119.D 120.A 121.C 122.B 123.A 124.A 125.D 126.B 127.A 128.B 129.D 130.B
Part 6: 131.B 132.A 133.A 134.C 135.D 136.B 137.A 138.B 139.D 140.D 141.C 142.D 143.D 144.B 145.B 146.C

Vocabulary Development for Test 1
(Reading part 7)
Ex.A.: 1.A 2.B 3.A 4.B
Ex.B.: 5.C 6.A 7.B
Ex.C.: 8. Defrost 9. inserts 10. liaison

Part 7: 147.C 148.D 149.A 150.C 151.A 152.A 153.A 154.D 155.B 156.D 157.B 158.D 159.D 160.D 161.C 162.C 163.B 164.C 165.C 166.B 167.B 168.A 169.D 170.C 171.B 172.A 173.C 174.B 175.C 176.B 177.B 178.B 179.A 180.A 181.C 182.C 183.D 184.B 185.B 186.A 187.D 188.B 189.C 190.B 191.B 192.A 193.C 194.D 195.D 196.B 197.D 198.B 199.B 200.D

TEST 2

LISTENING – Section 1

Part 1: 1.C 2.D 3.B 4.A 5.B 6.A
Part 2: 7.C 8.B 9.C 10.C 11.A 12.C 13.B 14.B 15.A 16.B 17.A 18.A 19.B 20.C 21.C 22.B 23.B 24.C 25.B 26.A 27.C 28.A 29.B 30.C 31.B
Part 3: 32.D 33.B 34.A 35.C 36.A 37.A 38.D 39.C 40.A 41.C 42.C 43.B 44.A 45.C 46.D 47.B 48.C 49.A 50.A 51.D 52.C 53.C 54.B 55.D 56.A 57.C 58.A 59.C 60.C 61.B 62.A 63.C 64.D 65.C 66.D 67.B 68.D 69.A 70.A
Part 4: 71.D 72.C 73.C 74.C 75.A 76.B 77.A 78.D 79.C 80.C 81.D 82.A 83.A 84.B 85.C 86.C 87.B 88.D 89.C 90.B 91.D 92.B 93.B 94.C 95.B 96.D 97.C 98.C 99.B 100.B

Vocabulary Development for Test 2
(Reading parts 5-6)
Ex.A.: 1.B 2.A 3.B 4.A
Ex.B.: 5.A 6.C 7.C
Ex.C.: 8. cutback 9. detrimental 10. ambiguous

READING – Section 2

Part 5: 101.C 102.B 103.C 104.A 105.D 106.C 107.D 108.C 109.A 110.D 111.D 112.A 113.A 114.B 115.C 116.A 117.C 118.C 119.D 120.A 121.C 122.B 123.C 124.C 125.A 126.A 127.C 128.C 129.D 130.A
Part 6: 131.C 132.D 133.A 134.C 135.C 136.D 137.C 138.C 139.C 140.D 141.B 142.A 143.B 144.A 145.B 146.C

Vocabulary Development for Test 2
(Reading part 7)
Ex.A.: 1.C 2.A 3.C 4.A
Ex.B.: 5.A 6.C 7.A
Ex.C.: 8. sustained 9. representative 10. discretion

Part 7: 147.A 148.C 149.B 150.C 151.A 152.C 153.C 154.A 155.D 156.B 157.A 158.A 159.B 160.D 161.A 162.C 163.A 164.B 165.C 166.D 167.B 168.A 169.B 170.A 171.D 172.D 173.D 174.A 175.B 176.D 177.D 178.C 179.A 180.B 181.B 182.B 183.A 184.A 185.D 186.B 187.B 188.A 189.D 190.C 191.C 192.A 193.A 194.C 195.D 196.B 197.A 198.A 199.A 200.C

TEST 3

LISTENING – Section 1

Part 1: 1.C 2.B 3.A 4.D 5.C 6.D
Part 2: 7.B 8.C 9.A 10.B 11.A 12.C 13.B 14.A 15.B 16.C 17.A 18.A 19.B 20.A 21.B 22.B 23.A 24.C 25.A 26.B 27.A 28.C 29.C 30.A 31.B
Part 3: 32.B 33.D 34.C 35.C 36.A 37.C 38.A 39.A 40.B 41.D 42.B 43.B 44.A 45.C 46.D 47.C 48.B 49.B 50.D 51.A 52.B 53.D 54.B 55.C 56.C 57.D 58.A 59.C 60.C 61.A 62.C 63.B 64.A 65.B 66.A 67.D 68.C 69.C 70.B
Part 4: 71.A 72.C 73.B 74.D 75.B 76.A 77.B 78.D 79.A 80.C 81.B 82.D 83.C 84.D 85.A 86.A 87.D 88.B 89.D 90.A 91.B 92.C 93.D 94.B 95.A 96.B 97.D 98.D 99.B 100.C

Vocabulary Development for Test 3
(Reading parts 5-6)
Ex.A.: 1.A 2.B 3.B 4.C
Ex.B.: 5.A 6.B 7.C
Ex.C.: 8. immense 9. surrogate 10. cockeyed

READING – Section 2

Part 5: 101.B 102.C 103.A 104.C 105.B 106.B 107.C 108.A 109.A 110.B 111.A 112.D 113.D 114.C 115.A 116.B 117.D 118.C 119.B 120.A 121.B 122.C 123.D 124.A 125.C 126.A 127.C 128.B 129.A 130.B
Part 6: 131.A 132.C 133.C 134.D 135.C 136.B 137.A 138.B 139.C 140.B 141.B 142.A 143.A 144.D 145.C 146.A

Vocabulary Development for Test 3
(Reading part 7)
Ex.A.: 1.A 2.C 3.B 4.C
Ex.B.: 5.A 6.C 7.B
Ex.C.: 8. leaped/leapt 9. incompatible 10. rigorous

Part 7: 147.C 148.B 149.D 150.B 151.A 152.D 153.C 154.B 155.C 156.D 157.A 158.A 159.C 160.C 161.A 162.C 163.D 164.B 165.D 166.B 167.D 168.A 169.B 170.B 171.D 172.B 173.B 174.C 175.A 176.C 177.A 178.A 179.B 180.C 181.D 182.C 183.B 184.A 185.B 186.D 187.D 188.A 189.C 190.B 191.B 192.C 193.A 194.C 195.B 196.A 197.C 198.A 199.C 200.B